THE HIDDEN COST OF FEDERAL TAX POLICY

The Hidden Cost of
Federal Tax Policy

JASON J. FICHTNER & JACOB M. FELDMAN

MERCATUS CENTER
George Mason University

Arlington, Virginia

ABOUT THE MERCATUS CENTER AT GEORGE MASON UNIVERSITY

The Mercatus Center at George Mason University is the world's premier university source for market-oriented ideas—bridging the gap between academic ideas and real-world problems.

A university-based research center, Mercatus advances knowledge about how markets work to improve people's lives by training graduate students, conducting research, and applying economics to offer solutions to society's most pressing problems.

Our mission is to generate knowledge and understanding of the institutions that affect the freedom to prosper and to find sustainable solutions that overcome the barriers preventing individuals from living free, prosperous, and peaceful lives.

Founded in 1980, the Mercatus Center is located on George Mason University's Arlington campus.

Mercatus Center at George Mason University
3434 Washington Blvd., 4th Floor
Arlington, Virginia 22201
www.mercatus.org

Library of Congress Cataloging-in-Publication Data

Fichtner, Jason J.
    The hidden cost of federal tax policy / by Jason J. Fichtner and Jacob M. Feldman. — 1 Edition.
        pages cm
    Includes index.
    ISBN 978-1-942951-10-0 (pbk.) — ISBN 978-1-942951-11-7 (kindle ebook)

1. Fiscal policy—United States.   2. Taxation—United States.
I. Feldman, Jacob M.   II. Title.
    HJ257.3.F58 2015
    336.200973—dc23
                                                        2015009193

CONTENTS

ABBREVIATIONS

ADS	alternative depreciation system
AMT	alternative minimum tax
CBO	Congressional Budget Office
EITC	earned income tax credit
GDP	gross domestic product
IRS	Internal Revenue Service
MACRS	modified accelerated cost-recovery system
MID	mortgage interest deduction
OECD	Organisation for Economic Co-operation and Development
R&D	research and development
TRA86	Tax Reform Act of 1986
VAT	value-added tax

INTRODUCTION
What Are the Goals of Tax Policy?

The most basic goal of tax policy is to raise enough revenue to meet the government's spending requirements in the way that has the least impact on market behavior.[1] But the US tax code has long failed to meet this aim: by distorting market decisions and the allocation of resources, the tax code hampers job creation and impedes both potential economic growth and potential tax revenue. This book does not distinguish tax provisions in terms of "good" or "bad" policy. Instead, it sets forth a general framework for evaluating any tax provision and delineates key problems existing within the tax code today.

To increase employment and expand their economies, most developed countries are both reducing their corporate tax rates and restructuring their tax systems to make them simpler. The United States appears to be taking the opposite approach. Dozens of tax provisions set to expire every year are extended repeatedly in a seemingly endless cycle. This process is evidence of the tax code's complex and temporary nature—two faults that increase both uncertainty and costs for American people and businesses. As we discuss in chapter 1, the costs of tax compliance may be nearly a trillion dollars annually in cumulative accounting costs, economic losses, and lobbying expenditures.

Although the need for major tax reform is widely recognized, there is no consensus—either between or within the political parties—on the specific elements of reform. To move the debate forward, policymakers need to understand the goals of successful tax reform and what steps to take to achieve those goals.

Clearly, the nation's economic and fiscal situation has increased the motivation—and the urgency—to reform the federal tax revenue system, along with the federal government's other unsustainable institutions and practices. But what would an ideal tax code look like?

Luckily, policymakers need not fly blind when it comes to defining the principles and goals key to a successful revenue system. Academic research suggests that a successful system should be simple, equitable, efficient, permanent, and predictable. We explore these themes in the chapters that follow.

Some have claimed the Tax Reform Act of 1986 (TRA86) is model legislation for what future tax reform should be. TRA86 was remarkable for its broad bipartisan support in Congress and for its sweeping reforms. But because the legislation failed to fix the revenue system's large institutional problems, the reforms were clawed back almost immediately. As a result, the tax code looks even worse today. For example, in 1985, there were only 25 temporary tax provisions; in 2010, 141 provisions were set to expire by the end of 2012.[2] Chapter 2, "What Can Be Learned from the Tax Reform Act of 1986?," provides key insights into why the act was considered one of the most successful tax reforms in US history—and also one of the biggest failures. One key lesson is that keeping the tax code as simple—by taxing a broad base at the same low rate—and as transparent as possible will help reduce the ability and incentives to reverse future tax reforms.[3]

One thing policymakers should not do is raise tax rates. There is much research to support the negative consequences of raising tax rates on economic growth. Research by Christina Romer, former chair of President Obama's Council of Economic Advisers, and David Romer, an economist at the University of California–Berkeley, suggests, "A tax increase of 1 percent of GDP reduces output over the next three years by nearly 3 percent."[4] Furthermore, according to research by Harvard University economist Jeffrey Miron, "Both macroeconomic and microeconomic perspectives suggest that [higher] taxes slow economic growth, thereby limiting the scope for revenue gains."[5] To regain competitiveness, the United States should reduce its corporate tax rate to 25 percent at most, the average rate of other Organisation for Economic Co-operation and Development countries. Chapter 3, "Why Should Congress Restructure the Corporate Income Tax?," examines trends in international corporate tax rates and discusses why the United States needs to lower the corporate tax rate to increase competitiveness.

Those who advocate for higher taxes on business should note two things. First, the statutory corporate tax rate in the United States is among the highest in the industrial world—a factor that encourages businesses to move to lower-tax countries, taking jobs, money, and tax dollars with them. Second, a tax on corporations is actually a tax on labor. A Congressional Budget Office working paper finds that "domestic labor bears slightly more than 70 percent of the burden of the corporate income tax."[6] Chapter 4, "Why Do Workers Bear a Significant Share of the Corporate Income Tax?," concludes that key pieces of the burden in today's modern open economy are borne by labor rather than by the owners of capital.

As discussed in chapter 5, "How Does the Corporate Tax Code Distort Capital Investments?," the current US tax code is complex—carved up by special interests and full of distortionary tax rates that treat similar activities unequally. Unequal taxation inefficiently distorts consumer and investor decisions, which can be damaging to the economy. These problems are particularly egregious regarding the tax rules applied to corporate capital investments. The tax code requires that most new purchases of capital, such as machines and buildings, be deducted from total revenue over the course of many years. This provision is called *depreciation*, or *capital cost recovery*. Unequal tax rates develop across industries because of disparities in when the tax is paid. A one-dollar investment today can be reduced to as little as 37 cents of its real write-off value, thereby diminishing the profitability of investments.[7] As shown in chapter 5, moving away from complex depreciation schedules toward full expensing can be one of many necessary tools to move toward a better tax system.

Consumer advocates view the mortgage interest deduction (MID) as a benefit for lower- and middle-income taxpayers.[8] Yet in chapter 6, "Why Should Congress Reform the Mortgage Interest Deduction?," data are presented that show that fewer than 9.8 percent of tax filers earning less than $50,000 claim the MID, and this group comprises the very same households that would gain the most from the sociological benefits of homeownership. In fact, most of the dollar benefits from the MID go to high-income earners whose average tax benefit from the deduction is nearly nine times greater than that of households earning $50,000 to $100,000. The chapter concludes that reforming the MID is essential to both increasing homeownership and properly aligning the deduction's policy goals with actual outcomes.

Allowing any tax provisions that favor one group or activity over others only puts the government in the position of picking winners and losers. Chapter 7, "How Do People Respond to the Marriage Tax Penalty?," provides a key example of unequal taxation among couples whose only differing characteristic is their marital status. For low-income taxpayers, the marriage tax penalty is a formidable barrier to the social benefits of marriage, while married high-income taxpayers are often discouraged from working.

History has shown that tax reforms seldom last when special interests have substantial incentives to lobby Congress for tax breaks. This book concludes that the current US tax code is detrimental to the economy. The US tax system severely distorts market decisions and the allocation of resources. It hampers job creation and impedes both potential economic growth and potential tax revenue. Tax expenditures also set up a system that allows the government to discriminate among taxpayers by picking winners and losers. Provisions and reforms that level the playing field should be promoted over rules that discriminate.

CHAPTER 1

What Are the Hidden Costs of Tax Compliance?

T he US tax code, far beyond simply collecting revenue to fund the operations of the federal government, attempts to perform policy and political functions as well. This chapter does not examine the normative value of these provisions but instead examines the hidden costs of the federal tax code: time and money spent submitting tax forms, forgone economic growth, lobbying expenditures, and gaps in revenue collection. These problems grow larger as the Internal Revenue Code becomes more complicated and temporary.[1] On the basis of the studies reviewed in this chapter, we estimate that hidden costs range from $215 billion to $987 billion annually and that the tax code results in a $452 billion revenue gap in unreported taxes (see table 1.1). For calendar year 2012 alone, the economic costs were substantial relative to the $2.45 trillion in revenue raised by the federal government.[2]

The structure of individual and corporate income taxes in the United States—accounting for over 55 percent of total tax revenue—reflects policymakers' agglomerated attempts to increase fairness, conduct social policy, encourage economic growth,

Table 1.1. Hidden Costs and Revenue Implications of the US Tax Code

HIDDEN COSTS		REVENUE IMPLICATIONS	
Accounting costs	$67 billion–$378 billion	Tax gap	$452 billion
Economic costs	$148 billion–$609 billion		

Note: Lobbying costs are another form of hidden costs; however, because a specific annual cost could not be approximated, they are not included here.

and promote favored industries.[3] According to the National Taxpayer Advocate, between 2001 and 2010 there were 4,428 changes to the Internal Revenue Code, including an estimated 579 changes in 2010 alone.[4] In other words, the tax code averages more than one change per day. The complexity of the tax code is largely responsible for the $67 billion to $378 billion in annual accounting costs incurred by taxpayers in the process of filing their tax returns. A simpler tax code with fewer deductions would assist in alleviating these costs.

Revenue collected by the federal government through taxes prevents economic transactions from occurring. The economic size of the purchases and business deals that do not occur is larger than the total revenue collected by the federal government. Net estimates of annual forgone economic growth range from $148 billion to $609 billion (see table 1.3, page 20).

Along with both accounting and economic costs, lobbying costs are a third cost of the existing US tax code. Although we do not have a full and complete estimate of annual lobbying costs to petition federal, state, and local governments for policy preferences, $27.6 billion was spent on reportable lobbying activities between 2002 and 2011 (see figure 1.2, page 25). More significantly for long-term economic growth, rather than providing an incentive for innovation, a tax code that is open to lobbyists encourages the pursuit of rent-seeking careers to protect and expand tax advantages.[5]

Finally, although it is not an economic cost, the structure of the federal tax code affects the government's ability to raise revenue efficiently and equitably. The United States has a tax-reporting compliance rate of 85.5 percent—leaving an estimated revenue gap of $452 billion in unreported taxes.[6] The government's failure to collect all revenue owed by law creates a social cost of inequitable tax burdens among similar taxpayers.[7] Policymakers who want to increase revenue for the federal government need to understand the risks and benefits that taxpayers assume by not reporting all taxable income. One case study based on the Russian economy suggests that shifting the US tax code to a flat tax holds promise for reducing the revenue gap.[8]

The extent to which many of these costs could be reduced quantitatively by tax code reform is beyond the scope of this chapter. The purpose here is to use the relevant scholarly literature to document the true costs of the US tax system. Later in the chapter, we provide qualitative recommendations based on successful tax reform in Russia and on the 1986 Tax Reform Act in the United States. Tax reform today must negate the incentives for both legal and illegal tax sheltering. Curtailing the hidden costs of taxation will require a simpler tax code with lower rates.

HOW THE TAX CODE INDUCES ACCOUNTING EXPENSES AND CREATES ECONOMIC DISTORTIONS

The federal government assesses personal income taxes on citizens or resident aliens on the basis of their worldwide adjusted gross income.[9] Individuals may reduce their tax liability by taking advantage of the personal exemption deductions[10] and the applicable standard deduction,[11] or they may join the 32 percent of taxpayers who choose the complicated and costly process of itemizing specific deductions.[12] Claiming tax deductions increases the accounting costs of filing tax returns, as well the economic costs caused by distortions in the price system. Determining tax liability for a given year may then be further complicated by the necessity of complying with the alternative minimum tax.[13] Later in this chapter, we quantify the financial and time costs of complying with the many deductions—approximately $378 billion. Each itemized deduction targets a specific set of taxpayer characteristics or a specific policy objective. The itemized deductions allowed, as well as their value, vary from tax year to tax year. As detailed in figure 1.1, in 2011 the 173 different tax deductions and credits for individuals and corporations amounted to about 7 percent of GDP. The numerous existing personal and corporate federal tax provisions have implications for economic growth in that they affect individual prosperity and the inter-

Figure 1.1. Growth in Federal Tax Expenditures, 1975–2013

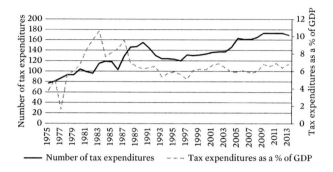

Source: Based on data from Office of Management and Budget, *Fiscal Year 2015 Analytical Perspectives, Budget of the US Government* (Washington, DC: Government Printing Office, March 4, 2014).

national competitiveness of American businesses— decreasing economic welfare by an estimated $148 billion to $609 billion annually (see table 1.3, page 20).

Unlike most industrial countries and all other members of the Group of Seven, the United States taxes all corporate income, regardless of where in the world it was generated. As a result, the current corporate tax structure discourages money earned abroad from being reinvested in the United States.[14] Foreign-source income is subject to taxation under the US tax code only when it is repatriated, or brought back to the United States.[15] Under this country's worldwide tax system, active income generated in a foreign country is subject to taxation under the US corporate tax code even after being taxed by the foreign government. To slightly reduce the negative effect of double taxation, the US tax code allows income tax paid to a foreign country where income is earned to be deducted from a corporation's US tax liability. But the US tax code provides a strong incentive for American corporations to retain earnings overseas instead of paying them out as dividends to shareholders or reinvesting the earnings here.

The structure of the US tax code cultivates unequal competition opportunities between large and small companies. As in all industrial nations, an American corporation may deduct from its income tax liability all expenditures needed to undertake its activities, including interest payments on any debt. However, although interest payments on corporate debt are deductible, returns to equity (shareholders' earnings) are taxed at the corporate tax rate. This feature of the US corporate tax code biases the financing decisions of businesses toward using debt financing rather than equity financing.[16] As a consequence, businesses are prone to being highly leveraged. Small businesses and less well-established businesses, which have more limited access to debt financing, are thus at a competitive disadvantage.

In addition to differences in competitive advantage based on access to corporate debt, small businesses are not as well equipped as large businesses to take advantage of complex depreciation schedules. In other circumstances, multinational companies engage in transfer-pricing activities through affiliates for tax purposes rather than for efficiency reasons. The documentation of sales from controlled affiliates in foreign countries to a larger American parent company may be adjusted to reduce tax liabilities. Even among large businesses, certain industries are able to take advantage of tax provisions while others languish under the high US corporate tax rates.[17] Larger businesses may deduct a capital investment over a number of years, subject to a complex depreciation schedule, whereas smaller businesses may deduct capital purchases at the time of investment. As a result, the after-tax cost of investments by larger businesses increases, because a dollar of spending today is more expensive than a dollar of spending in the future. On top of this complex system of deductions, depreciation, and liabilities, there are other deductions and benefits for favored industries or taxpayers perceived to perform socially beneficial functions. For example, Robert Dietz, assistant vice president for tax and policy issues for the National Association of Home Builders, argues that favorable tax treatment for homeownership lowers crime rates and provides varied personal benefits.[18] Such a complex system of taxation, however, imposes a compliance cost on individuals and corporations in addition to the missed economic growth opportunities.

COMPLYING WITH COMPLEXITY

Under the US tax system, which is enforced primarily through voluntary compliance, it is the taxpayer's obligation to compute and pay federal taxes to the IRS. Voluntary tax compliance is achieved through countless hours of taxpayer efforts, often with the help of paid tax consultants. The accounting costs of complying with the US tax code range from $67 billion to $378 billion (see table 1.2).

Table 1.2. Studies on the Costs of Taxation

STUDY	ANNUAL COMPLIANCE COSTS	IMPORTANT DIFFERENCES IN SCOPE AND ASSUMPTIONS	NOTABLE METHODOLOGICAL ISSUES
Guyton, O'Hare, Stavrianos, and Toder (2003) Year of data: Tax year 2000	$67 billion–$99 billion for individuals (Individual taxpayers experienced a total compliance burden of 3.21 billion hours and $18.8 billion.)[a]	• This study covers taxpayers' time, preparers' fees, and any other out-of-pocket expenses. • Taxpayers' time is monetized at $15 per hour for the low estimate and $25 per hour for the high estimate.	• This study is based on surveys of two samples of taxpayers: one (in 2000) of individuals who earned only wage and investment income and the second (in 2001) for self-employed individuals.
Slemrod (2004) Year of data: Tax year 2004	$85 billion for individuals	• This study covers taxpayers' time, preparers' fees, and any other out-of-pocket expenses. • Taxpayers' time is monetized at $20 per hour.	• This study is based on the author's informed judgment of accumulated research on this topic, including his own study of a sample of Minnesota taxpayers in 1989 (with Marsha Blumenthal)[b] and the Guyton et al. (2003) study.

Study	Estimate	Notes	
Moody, Warcholik, and Hodge (2006) Year of data: Calendar year 2005	$111 billion for individuals, $148 billion for businesses, and $7 billion for nonprofits	• This study covers tax-payers' time, preparers' fees, and any other out-of-pocket expenses. • Taxpayers' time is monetized at $39.18 per hour for individuals and $47.96 per hour for businesses and nonprofits.	• This study covers taxpayers' estimated paperwork burden. • The study is based on data from an IRS survey of taxpayers for tax year 1983; the methodology for updating the data is simplistic and does not account for changes in tax preparation and recordkeeping technology.
Laffer, Winegarden, and Childs (2011) Year of data: Tax year 2008	$378 billion total: $216 billion for individuals and $162 billion for businesses	• This study covers taxpayers' time;[c] individuals' time is monetized at $68.42 per hour and businesses' time at $55 per hour. • When preparers' fees and IRS administrative costs are included, Laffer, Winegarden, and Childs estimate that the total cost of tax compliance is potentially upward of $431 billion.	• The average income used to monetize taxpayers' time is significantly greater than the average income used in other estimates. The authors note that this difference is due to their use of a weighted average, which accounts for the fact that low-income taxpayers pay less in taxes.

(continued)

Table 1.2. (*continued*)

Sources: John L. Guyton, John F. O'Hare, Michael P. Stavrianos, and Eric J. Toder, "Estimating the Compliance Cost of the U.S. Individual Income Tax," presented at the 33rd National Tax Association Spring Symposium, Washington, DC, May 29–30, 2003; Joel Slemrod, Written testimony submitted to the Committee on Ways and Means, Subcommittee on Oversight, Hearing on Tax Simplification, Washington, DC, June 15, 2004; J. Scott Moody, Wendy P. Warcholik, and Scott A. Hodge, "The Rising Cost of Complying with the Federal Income Tax," Tax Foundation, Washington, DC, Special Report 138, December 2005; Arthur B. Laffer, Wayne H. Winegarden, and John Childs, *The Economic Burden Caused by Tax Code Complexity,* Laffer Center, Austin, TX, April 2011.

a. Guyton et al. adjusted their estimates in accordance with the reduced compliance time estimated by the IRS.

b. See Marsha Blumenthal and Joel Slemrod, "The Compliance Cost of the U.S. Individual Income Tax System: A Second Look after Tax Reform," *National Tax Journal* 45, no. 2 (June 1992): 185–202.

c. The IRS estimates that individuals spent 6.1 billion hours in 2008 complying with filing requirements: 3.16 billion hours for individuals and 2.94 billion hours for businesses. The IRS provides its own compliance cost estimates. On the basis of the average hourly cost of a civilian employee, the IRS Taxpayer Advocate Service estimates that the costs of complying with the individual and corporate income tax requirements in 2008 were $163 billion, which is equivalent to 11 percent of aggregate income tax receipts. See Taxpayer Advocate Service, *National Taxpayer Advocate 2010 Annual Report to Congress,* vol. 1 (Washington, DC: IRS, 2010). Laffer, Winegarden, and Childs (2011) adjust the IRS numbers upward because the IRS does not adequately account for the skewed nature of the tax complexity burden toward higher-income earners. The weighted average hourly income used by Laffer, Winegarden, and Childs for each individual's time is $68.42. For businesses, the labor expense is estimated at $55 per hour for a tax accountant and is based on a weighted average annual salary, with bonuses and benefits, of $102,184.50 (plus the employer portion of FICA).

About 60 percent of individual taxpayers and 71 percent of unincorporated business taxpayers hire others—accountants, lawyers, tax professionals—to prepare their tax returns.[19] An additional 32 percent of individual taxpayers use tax preparation software to complete their tax returns.[20] As a direct result of the large and growing complexity of the US tax code, the vast majority of Americans now incur some type of monetary expense to determine their income tax liability and to comply with filing requirements.

Furthermore, some taxpayers venture to contact the IRS directly with questions regarding their income tax liability. In 2012, the IRS website received more than 1.7 billion page views. The agency also received 115 million phone calls in each of fiscal years 2011 and 2012—and more than 30 percent of those phone calls were not answered.[21] The agency was able to answer only 68 percent of phone calls in 2012, compared with 87 percent in 2004.[22] Additionally, the IRS failed to respond, within the agency's own established time frame, to almost half (48 percent) of all taxpayers' letters, up drastically from 12 percent in 2004.[23] In September 2011, the Treasury Department inspector general's semiannual report to Congress found that most taxpayers who had contacted the IRS had not received "quality" responses to their correspondence. The report cited a review of three IRS functions—Accounts Management, Automated Underreporter Program, and Field Assistance Office—and noted that 19 percent, 56 percent, and 8 percent, respectively, of correspondents received timely and accurate responses to their questions.[24]

On the basis of costs incurred by taxpayers in terms of personal time and estimated direct outlays for products and services used to determine their federal income tax liability, several economists have formulated empirical estimates of the cost of tax compliance (see table 1.2). These estimates, though not comprehensive, suggest that the direct costs of tax compliance are substantial, particularly relative to the actual amount of revenue raised.[25]

The staggering costs of tax compliance efforts by individuals and businesses are well illustrated in a 2011 study by Laffer, Winegarden, and Childs.[26] The study estimates that taxpayers spent $378 billion in compliance costs in 2008—an amount that exceeds the profits of the 25 largest American corporations.[27] Similarly, an estimated 6.1 billion hours spent annually on efforts to comply with income tax forms represents an annual workforce of over 3.4 million people—a population surpassing that of Chicago, the third-largest city in the United States, which has only 2,707,120 residents.[28] This workforce is larger than the populations of 21 states. Even the four largest American companies combined employ only slightly more workers (Wal-Mart Stores, 2.2 million; IBM, 433,000; McDonald's, 420,000; and Target, 365,000).[29] And these administrative tax costs reveal only the more easily measured surface costs of federal income taxes. The true cost of tax compliance far exceeds taxpayers' documented personal time and financial expenses. The remainder of this chapter addresses three other costs of taxation: lobbying efforts to gain and maintain tax advantages; economy-wide costs, as a result of work, leisure, savings, consumption, production, and investments being altered by tax incentives; and revenue lost as a result of taxpayer noncompliance. Several recommendations are given to lessen the hidden costs of taxation.

THE COSTS OF TAX AVOIDANCE

Tax avoidance occurs when individuals or businesses reallocate consumption and saving patterns to minimize tax burdens. Behavioral responses to tax avoidance result in what economists call *decreased allocative efficiency*—a loss of economic transactions that would increase standards of living, such as vacations not taken, food not purchased, and less expensive gifts purchased. In other words, consumers make smaller spending and saving decisions than they would otherwise.[30] Estimates of economic growth lost annually as a result of taxes range from $148 billion to $609 billion (see table 1.3). Taxes increase the cost of doing business—buying materials, paying workers, making investments. Businesses sell fewer products and services in response to resources shifting to the next-best social function. The extent to which the federal tax code distorts business decisions may be thought of in terms of whether consumption is penalized relative to saving. Additionally, different forms of saving may be penalized or rewarded relative to one another. If individuals or businesses are unsure how

Table 1.3. Studies on the Costs of Deadweight Loss

STUDY	DEADWEIGHT LOSS
Harberger (1964) Year of data: 1964	The study calculates $14 billion annually for federal income taxes. Estimate does not include the effect of payroll taxes. Loss is equal to 2.5 percent of revenue raised.
Feldstein (1999)[a] Years of data: 1994, 2012	For 1994, the study estimates $181 billion for federal income taxes without payroll taxes and $284 billion with payroll taxes. Loss is equal to 32.2 percent of the computer program TAXSIM's estimate of personal income tax revenue ($543 billion). Feldstein calculates that the marginal deadweight loss per tax dollar was $2.06. For 2012, deadweight loss is estimated at $388 billion without payroll taxes and $609 billion with payroll taxes.[b]
Blomquist and Simula (2012) Years of data: 1994, 2012	For 1994, $69 billion is estimated after accounting for federal income taxes with payroll taxes and for state income and sales taxes. Blomquist and Simula find a marginal deadweight loss per tax dollar of $1.35. For 2012, deadweight loss is estimated at $148 billion after accounting for federal income taxes with payroll taxes and for state income and sales taxes.[c]
Chetty (2009)	Deadweight loss is less than contemporary estimates because of the material costs necessary to dodge taxes. Some deadweight loss is actually a payment for services rendered for income to be sheltered from taxation. As a result, these transactions do materialize, although they would not be necessary under a simplified tax code.

(*continued*)

Table 1.3. (*continued*)

Sources: Arnold C. Harberger, "Taxation, Resource Allocation, and Welfare," in *The Role of Direct and Indirect Taxes in the Federal Reserve System*, ed. John Due, 25–80 (Princeton, NJ: Princeton University Press, 1964); Martin Feldstein, "Tax Avoidance and the Deadweight Loss of the Income Tax," *Review of Economics and Statistics* 81, no. 4 (1999): 674–80; Sören Blomquist and Laurent Simula, "Marginal Deadweight Loss When the Income Tax Is Nonlinear," Uppsala University and Uppsala Center for Fiscal Studies, Uppsala, Sweden, March 8, 2012; Raj Chetty, "Is the Taxable Income Elasticity Sufficient to Calculate Deadweight Loss? The Implications of Evasion and Avoidance," *American Economic Journal: Economic Policy* 1, no. 2 (August 2009): 31–52; Office of Management and Budget, "Receipts by Source as Percentages of GDP: 1934–2017," table 2.1, http://www.whitehouse.gov/sites/default/files/omb/budget/fy2013/assets/hist02z1.xls.
a. Harberger's (1964) approach is applied in Feldstein's (1999) paper to 1994 data.
b. Estimate is based on data from Office of Management and Budget, table 2.1, "Receipts by Source as Percentages of GDP: 1934–2017," http://www.whitehouse.gov/sites/default/files/omb/budget/fy2013/assets/hist02z1.xls
c. This estimate assumes the ratio of deadweight loss to federal income tax revenues is fixed. The Office of Management and Budget has applied this ratio to estimated data for 2012 in an effort to estimate deadweight loss for that year. However, the data are more complex than this rough estimation shows, because the elasticity of taxable income may be calculated differently than Friedman calculated it in 1999.

the tax code will affect returns on investment, they may put off investing until more certainty exists.[31] Investments that do not occur because they are prohibitively expensive—an implicit result of taxation—slow economic growth.

Economists have a term for forgone investments and consumption—*deadweight loss,* an idea that gained prominence from the work of Arnold Harberger in the 1960s.[32] More recently, Martin Feldstein builds on Harberger's work with his own methodology and finds that deadweight loss in general is higher than Harberger anticipated because tax rates are not applied evenly between spending and saving choices.[33] Examining 1994 data on income taxes, Feldstein estimates that deadweight loss to revenue was 12 times larger than Harberger's estimate. Feldstein estimates that 1994 deadweight loss from federal income taxes was $181 billion, or 2.55 percent of GDP, which would equal approximately $388 billion in 2012. In 2008, Feldstein reexamined deadweight loss by using an estimated compensated elasticity of 0.4, given the existing US tax code.[34]

With 124 special deductions and credits in the 1994 federal tax code (there were 173 in 2011), there was a menu of effective rates for businesses and individuals to shift resources toward to avoid higher tax liabilities. These deductions assisted businesses in equalizing some of their decisions about whether to save or consume. However, these deductions also further added to the federal tax code's complexity, which not only tied up other resources but also rendered better outcomes for businesses (often corporations) with professional tax compliance officers, while smaller businesses missed out on such opportunities.[35] Despite the highest level of deductions and credits in US history, the incentive to save versus consume is still treated unevenly in the tax code for many industries. It is clear that carving out special deductions and exemptions ties up far too many resources in the compliance process, favors larger businesses, and still does not achieve the goal of taxing both saving and consumption at equal rates.

In 2012, Uppsala University economists Sören Blomquist and Laurent Simula revisited Feldstein's analysis of deadweight loss by using a model that better resembles today's tax code (i.e., a nonlinear model). Blomquist and Simula claim theirs is a more accurate model because the US tax code is progressive, meaning that tax rates increase with income. Using the same datasets as Feldstein, Blomquist and Simula find that Feldstein's linear model overestimates marginal deadweight loss per tax dollar by 61 percent. Under the 2006 tax code, which had the same marginal income tax rates as the 2012 code, deadweight loss per tax dollar was 4.1 percent.[36] In 2006, deadweight loss totaled $98.7 billion, and if the same levels were applied to 2012 revenue, the total would be $100.4 billion.[37]

University of Nebraska–Lincoln economist Seth Giertz estimates a range of potential deadweight losses if all individual federal income tax rates were increased after expiration of the Bush-era tax cuts.[38] Giertz's numbers reveal that deadweight loss would fall to between 0.72 and 3.62 percent of GDP ($15.6 billion and $77.8 billion, respectively), depending on the elasticity of taxable income response ranging between 0.2 and 1.0.[39]

Another response to Feldstein—suggesting that deadweight losses were lower than his estimates—comes from UC–Berkeley economist Raj Chetty. He questions whether the efficiency cost of taxation for tax avoidance and tax evasion exhibits the same deadweight loss as marginal tax rates. Chetty emphasizes that tax evasion often exhibits different deadweight loss characteristics than tax avoidance does but that both may exhibit deadweight loss 40 percent smaller than that from marginal tax rates.[40] Tax avoidance is the act of using a legal method to reduce tax liability, such as using tax expenditures or not repatriating foreign earnings to the United States. Tax evasion is an illegal behavior—reducing tax burden by not reporting taxable earnings. Feldstein assumes that the decision to shelter income has a marginal cost rate similar to taxes. However, economists Joel Slemrod and Shlomo Yitzhaki explain that the US tax system sets the relative price of avoidance or evasion through the costs and benefits of "honesty."[41] Chetty argues that many forms of tax sheltering require resource costs lower than complying with the top marginal tax rates. Therefore, much of perceived deadweight loss is actually a transfer cost to shelter income.[42]

Although the costs of deadweight losses are difficult to estimate, policymakers can take steps to lessen the damage that does occur. A more complex tax code might lower deadweight losses slightly as long as marginal rates remain constant, because a more complex code also increases resources spent on tax preparation and lobbying efforts. An ideal tax code would be one in which deadweight losses remain low and resources spent on tax compliance are minimized. The policy recommendations presented later in this chapter examine contemporary solutions and historical responses. The next section examines the costs of lobbying.

Figure 1.2. Growth in Lobbying, 1998–2011

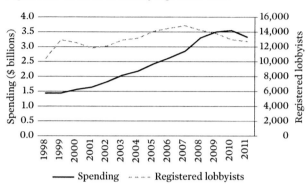

Source: OpenSecrets.org, Center for Responsive Politics, Lobbying Database, http://www.opensecrets.org/lobby/.

DIRECT COST OF GAINING AND PROTECTING CURRENT TAX ADVANTAGES

Lobbying costs are expenditures made by businesses to petition federal, state, and local governments for particular tax advantages. As shown in figure 1.2, between 2002 and 2011, $27.61 billion was spent on lobbying efforts. Although not all such spending is related to obtaining and protecting tax advantages for particular interests, empirical research has found a relationship between the two.

A 2009 study by political scientists Brian Richter, Krislert Samphantharak, and Jeffrey Timmons finds that resources spent on lobbying efforts yield high returns. Businesses that increased lobbying expenditures by 1 percent reduced their effective tax rates by 0.5 to 1.6 percentage points the following year. In nominal terms, an increase of approximately $7,800 in lobbying costs correlated with tax benefits of $4.8 million to $16 million. Including existing annual spending on lobbying efforts, each additional dollar spent on lobbying translated to $6 to $20 in tax benefits. Richter, Samphantharak, and Timmons also find that returns on lobbying efforts are relatively high compared to the investment, although the revenue cost to the federal government is somewhat modest.[43] Similarly, business professors Hui Chen, David Parsley, and Ya-Wen Yang find that lobbying expenditures positively correlate with financial performance. However, not all businesses benefit equally from the marginal unit of lobbying expenditures. Businesses with the highest levels of lobbying earned excess returns of 5.5 percent over three years following portfolio formation.[44]

Visible lobbying expenditures are, however, not the only costs of an "influenced" Congress. Other costs to a business include forgone investments and employment, given that financial resources are redistributed from creative entrepreneurship to rent-seeking behavior. As a result of lobbying costs, resources might, for example, be redistributed from the next engineering innovation to lawyers seeking to secure a slice of the existing economic pie. According to economists Kevin Murphy, Andrei Shleifer, and Robert Vishny, there is an international correlation between a reduction in a country's economic growth and an increase in the number of law students. Countries with robust economic growth have higher levels of students engaged in engineering studies. Murphy, Shleifer, and Vishny suggest that well-developed economies encourage rent-seeking rather than cultivate innovative careers.[45]

The durability of tax policy can also affect the pursuit of rent-seeking behavior. A 2012 paper by Seth Giertz and Jacob Feldman finds that uncertainty over which provisions the tax code will include correlates with a rise in rent-seeking behavior, particularly during the 21st century.[46] In some circumstances, industries may emerge in response to policy uncertainty. A 1994 study by Federico Sturzenegger and Mariano Tommasi finds that countries with unstable macroeconomic growth policies induced entrepreneurs to spend more time collecting information about decision-relevant variables, rather than going directly to production and investment. Evidence of growing rent-seeking behavior in these countries included a large financial sector in high-inflation economies, as well as growing information-gathering and policy-influencing activities. In short, when talent is allocated to influencing—that is, lobbying—rather than producing, economic growth stalls. The damage to businesses of resource misallocation can be diminished if the government acts to limit tax policy uncertainty. Sturzenegger and Tommasi claim that, "when winners and losers are clearly defined, the incentive to shift resources out of productive activities is much weaker."[47]

VISION OF A BETTER STATE

To achieve a stronger US economy and bring in higher tax revenue, tax code reform needs to simplify the economic and accounting burdens of complying with federal taxation requirements. The burdens of these costs often fall inequitably on smaller businesses and individual taxpayers. An overly complex and cumbersome tax code favors businesses and individuals who can afford well-paid accountants and lawyers. Both US history and international reforms should guide legislators toward how best to achieve a more productive and equitable federal tax revenue system.

During the Reagan administration, the Tax Reform Act of 1986 (TRA86) was enacted with significant bipartisan support. The act was important because it represented the first time in American history that a significant number of tax expenditures were removed from the tax code in exchange for reducing income tax rates on individuals. Although much of the act's successes had unraveled by the time of the 1993 Omnibus Act under the Clinton administration, there were some efficiency gains that reduced deadweight loss (see chapter 2). A 2007 paper by Federal Reserve Bank economist Anil Kumar finds that TRA86 reduced deadweight loss as a percentage of taxes by 6 percent. Combined with the positive labor effects of federal tax reform, Kumar estimates that an average male head of household was 10 percent better off after tax reform: "Before TRA 1986 an average male head would have been willing to pay about 28% of his Adjusted Gross Income to do away with the pre-TRA 1986 tax system. This figure drops to 25% after the tax reform—a drop of about 10%."[48]

Empirical literature suggests that income tax reform may diminish tax evasion but that reducing deadweight loss from tax avoidance may be more difficult. In a 2009 paper examining the 2001 Russian tax reform actions, economists Yuriy Gorodnichenko, Jorge Martinez-Vazquez, and Klara Peter find that welfare gains from adopting a flat tax were relatively low, whereas tax compliance improved significantly, with an additional 10 percent of reported income relative to consumption. These authors estimate that the deadweight loss effects of tax evasion are 30 percent lower than the deadweight loss effects of traditional income responses to tax changes. They conclude that two-thirds of the increase in taxable income may be attributable to reduced tax evasion, rather than increased productivity.[49]

Improved taxpayer compliance in the United States would have important implications for the federal government. According to the IRS, there was a compliance rate of 83.1 percent in 2006—which resulted in a revenue gap of $450 billion, or 3.36 percent of 2006 GDP.[50] After IRS enforcement, there was a net compliance rate of 85.5 percent. Hence, 14.5 percent of 2006 estimated tax liabilities could not be collected through IRS enforcement efforts—$385 billion, or 2.88 percent of GDP. In 2012 dollars, that percentage would be $452 billion in revenue.[51] In part, tax revenue not collected by the federal government may instead be used in ways that contribute to economic growth, which would offset economic loss caused by the tax code. However, some revenue that is shifted overseas is not reported to the IRS. Some studies estimate that the revenue cost to the federal government from individual and corporate overseas tax evasion ranges from $50 billion to $130 billion.[52] Tax reform intended to increase taxpayer compliance will require an understanding of the risks and costs of underreporting income.

University of Michigan economist Joel Slemrod notes that income tax evasion generates normative public policy problems, which this chapter does not address. First, evasion creates horizontal inequities because workers with equal earnings have different tax burdens. Second, evasion provides perverse social incentives for production activities where taxation is relatively light. An efficient tax code—and one that reduces the social costs of inequity—treats all production activities equally.[53]

Tax compliance costs in the United States are very high, and these costs have implications for lost economic growth, money spent unnecessarily on professional tax services, and even the collection of federal revenue. In 2011, individuals and businesses spent approximately $378 billion in time and for products and services to comply with the overly complex US tax code. For businesses, these resources would have been better spent on activities that increased capacity and production—and at the individual level, on work, saving, and investment. The US tax system may, in fact, have unintentionally thwarted approximately $148 billion of economic growth. Tax reform that reduces marginal tax rates may have a small and positive effect on national productivity. Finally, complying with higher marginal tax rates affects the federal government's ability to bring in needed revenue. The federal government may have missed out on approximately $452 billion in tax revenue in 2012 alone as a result of illegal evasion.[54]

As policymakers debate reforming the federal tax code, they should pay attention to the approximately $452 billion in uncollected revenue and the high-end estimate of almost $1 trillion from annual compliance, complexity, and economic costs associated with the current tax system.[55] Tax reform that reduces overall complexity will likely lead to greater efficiency, less paperwork, and higher tax revenue.

CHAPTER 2

What Can Be Learned from the Tax Reform Act of 1986?

This chapter provides an analysis of federal tax expenditures around the time of the Tax Reform Act of 1986 (TRA86) in conjunction with an examination of the contemporary US tax code. The analysis measures the effects of tax expenditures through the criteria of efficiency, equity, and simplicity. TRA86 was selected as a point of comparison with the contemporary tax code because it is generally considered the most successful effort, to date, to lower standard marginal tax rates and broaden the tax base through elimination of tax expenditures. However, many of the goals of TRA86 were not achieved, and even its few successes quickly unraveled. TRA86's temporary successes were undone by the income tax system's inherent nature to favor deductions and credits. At the time, TRA86's passage seemed like a great success for federal tax reform. The debate leading up to passage of TRA86 was contentious and, like today, major tax reform was considered politically impossible. Yet TRA86 garnered significant bipartisan support, with final passage in the Senate on a 97–3 vote. TRA86 achieved strong bipartisan support by improving three aspects of the tax code: efficiency, equity, and simplicity. All three goals were accomplished in some measure by reducing standard tax rates, increasing the standard deduction, and ending various tax expenditures that distributed resources to less efficient production purposes.

Looking at the tax code today, taxpayers would be hard pressed to find the aspects of efficiency, equity, and simplicity that were improved by TRA86. In contrast to the 25 expiring expenditures in the 1985 tax code, in 2010 some 141 provisions were due to expire within two years.[1] Tax expenditures have returned and multiplied in number since the enactment of TRA86 because the income tax system remains easily subject to capture by lobbyists and special interests. Still, in December 2014, Congress passed—and President Barack Obama signed into law—the Tax Increase Prevention Act of 2014, a temporary one-year retroactive extension of 50 popular tax provisions that had expired at the end of calendar year 2013.[2]

What has happened over the nearly 30 years since TRA86 became law? How quickly did the reforms of TRA86 unravel and why? This chapter examines the act's goals of efficiency, equity, and simplicity to find the failures and lasting successes of TRA86. Now, nearly 30 years later, the federal tax code is again in dire need of reform. The old saying that those who ignore history are doomed to repeat it applies to tax reform, too. Those who wish to reform the federal tax code today would be wise to learn from the past.

BACKGROUND: TAX EXPENDITURES
IN THE BUDGET PROCESS

Scholars disagree over what is and is not a tax expenditure.[3] What they do generally agree on is that tax expenditures obscure the size of government spending. Certain preferences in the US tax code are labeled tax expenditures because they are very similar to government spending. As Donald Marron, former acting director of the Congressional Budget Office, points out, "The rationale for viewing the preferences as expenditures, rather than mere tax breaks, was (and is) that their budgetary, economic, and distributional effects are often indistinguishable from those of spending programs."[4] Marron provides an exemplification originally offered by Princeton economist David Bradford:

> Suppose that policymakers wanted to slash defense procurement and reduce taxes, but did not want to undermine America's national security. They could square that circle by offering defense firms a refundable "weapons-supply tax credit" for producing desired weapons systems. The military would still get the weapons deemed essential to national security, defense contractors would get a tax cut, and politicians would get to boast about cutting both taxes and spending. But nothing would have changed meaningfully.[5]

Relying solely on government outlays (spending) as a measure of the size of the federal government underestimates its true and larger size by excluding tax expenditure items that should rightly be considered spending. Because many tax expenditures are best described as a form of subsidy, some spending programs receive a preemptive allocation of government resources and are effectively exempted from the competitive process of seeking scarce government outlays.[6] Nonetheless, in some cases, tax expenditures can be a useful mechanism for economic growth and can be preferable to federal outlays.

Not all particular aspects of the tax expenditure process produce suboptimal budgeting allocations. In 1994, tax law expert Edward Zelinsky published a paper on public choice and tax expenditures that defends the budget process. Zelinsky argues that the homogeneous orientation of nontax congressional committees made committee members more vulnerable to capture by rent-seekers, whereas the heterogeneous interests of the members of the House Ways and Means Committee and the Senate Finance Committee made them less vulnerable to capture.[7] In other words, when a congressional committee consists of members with like-minded interests, it is more prone to lobbying influence as a group than is a committee whose members have diverse interests. For example, according to Zelinsky's research, each member of the Senate Committee on Agriculture, Nutrition, and Forestry received on average more than seven times the campaign contributions as members of the Senate Finance Committee from agricultural political action committees. Moreover, outlays for agriculture clientele from the Senate Committee on Agriculture substantially exceeded tax expenditures.[8] Zelinsky concludes that the heterogeneous interests of tax-writing committees may better serve US interests in allocating federal subsidies.

However, Zelinsky's theory of rent-seeking does not address the budgetary consequences of tax expenditures. Paul McDaniel, director of the graduate tax program at New York University School of Law, finds that tax expenditures have been written on an ad hoc basis without regard to federal spending: "Tax expenditures are largely uncontrolled by the budget process because no effective limits are imposed on them. . . . [T]here is virtually no coordination between tax expenditures and actions by the authorization-appropriations committees in the same budget area."[9] In fact, tax-writing committees will overappropriate tax expenditures so that committee members can later claim to be tax cutters.[10]

Contrary to Zelinsky's theory that a diverse group of interests among members of congressional tax-writing committees will make members less prone to special-interest pressures, the ability to pass tax expenditures without counting them as spending gives committee members a "special status of a *Congress within the Congress*" that can determine its own spending policies while appearing to cut taxes.[11] Edward Kleinbard suggests that "the ever-increasing reliance on tax expenditures to deliver government programs is a symptom of an institutional weakness in the design of current federal budget processes."[12] The primary consequence of unchecked tax expenditures is that the size of government subsidization becomes obscured, and honest public policy conversations about the size of government are not straightforward. As Kleinbard writes, "Tax expenditures augment fiscal illusion, and fiscal illusion in turn drives poor policy."[13]

EFFICIENCY

With the enactment of TRA86, greater efficiency was achieved by eliminating tax expenditures and lowering the standard tax rate, but many additional potential gains were left untouched. Whether the provisions in the US tax code apply to corporations or to individuals, efficiency affects the salaries, jobs, and prices of goods and services across the country. Economists Jane Gravelle and Laurence Kotlikoff developed a model that found that TRA86's approach of broadening the corporate tax base and lowering the corporate tax rate reduces the annual excess burden of the US tax structure by $31 billion, based on the 1988 level of US consumption (equivalent to $61 billion in 2013).[14] By reducing the standard corporate tax rate and removing many special-preference items, TRA86 encouraged corporations to pursue a more efficient allocation of resources among production, investment, and payment of dividends. Unfortunately, loopholes for many special preferences, such as the investment tax credit and mortgage interest deduction, were untouched by TRA86 owing to popular political support and special-interest lobbying efforts. We now examine one temporary efficiency success of TRA86 before analyzing how and why the act's tax code cleanup efforts did not go far enough.

One primary success of TRA86 was to treat capital gains, dividends, and ordinary income more equitably by broadening the tax base and lowering the corporate standard tax rate. Equalizing these tax rates encourages businesses and individuals to pursue investment strategies that maximize long-term growth and productivity, rather than short-run gains from exploiting tax preferences. Prior to the enactment of TRA86, capital gains were taxed at a lower rate than corporate earnings. The preferential rate for capital gains created an incentive for businesses to retain earnings so as to drive up share prices and build up capital gains to save on their tax liability to shareholders. According to Don Fullerton and Yolanda Henderson, the efficient allocation of capital increased by 0.5 percent after TRA86 became law.[15]

Despite reforms to treat corporate assets more equally, TRA86 left one glaring corporate tax preference untouched. Research and development (R&D) expenditures continued to be taxed at effective rates that were lower than those applying to other assets as a result of a corporate R&D tax credit. Eliminating the investment tax credit without touching the R&D tax credit made investment in physical capital, production, and shareholder payouts relatively more expensive compared to R&D investment.[16] This tax credit overemphasized R&D by transforming previously subsidized investment in plant and equipment into R&D expenditures.

Inefficiency was a problem not only in the corporate sector but also for individual tax expenditures. One long-standing and significant example of inefficiency in the personal income tax is the mortgage interest deduction for owner-occupied housing. By making homeownership less expensive relative to other long-run capital assets, tax subsidization of homes artificially inflates the demand for and prices of housing across the country.[17] Calling it the last tax shelter, Douglas Holtz-Eakin, former director of the Congressional Budget Office, claims that "owner-occupied housing in the United States may grow at the expense of more productive investments elsewhere in the economy."[18] In testimony before the Senate Committee on Finance in September 2010 on lessons learned from TRA86, John Chapoton, assistant secretary for tax policy at the Department of Treasury during the Reagan administration, affirmed the inefficiency of the mortgage interest deduction and claimed that the tax expenditure is clearly a factor in the recent subprime mortgage crisis.[19]

By providing tax expenditures, the government allocates a significant amount of resources via the US tax code to many different sectors of the economy. Kleinbard writes:

> One discovers that our nondefense, non-safety net annual spending through tax subsidies is about 275 percent of the amount of explicit Government outlays in . . . education, transportation, scientific research, and every other activity by which the Federal Government touches the day-to-day lives of middle class and affluent Americans under the age of 65.[20]

Tax subsidies exist for many sectors of the economy. In 2013 alone, the health care industry received a tax subsidy of 1.1 percent of GDP for employee coverage (see table 2.1). In theory, each tax subsidy creates higher prices for the subsidized goods or services and causes a misallocation of resources as suppliers meet government-induced demand.[21]

Most of the items that the federal government lists as tax expenditures should be counted as spending because they violate equity by favoring specific activities; however, other items remove existing inequities created by the current tax code. For example, the exclusion of employer contributions for medical insurance premiums might be considered a tax expenditure that increases spending on health care, whereas the preferential treatment of capital gains is designed to offset some of the inequitable double taxation of capital gains that exists, because capital gains are taxed first at the corporate level and then again at the individual level. The taxation of capital gains is an important policy issue, but it is not spending disguised in the tax code.

Additionally, some items considered tax expenditures seemingly have no place in the tax code. Consider net imputed rental income. Many durable goods provide a flow of net value attributable to their consumption value. For example, a person who rents a house for a market price of $2,000 a month consumes $2,000 of housing per month. Now consider a person who purchased a house 10 years ago with a fixed 30-year mortgage payment of $1,500 per month. Assume this homeowner is able to rent the house at a market

Table 2.1. Ten Largest Individual Tax Expenditures

	2013 AMOUNT ($ MILLIONS)	SHARE OF GDP (%)
Exclusion of employer contributions for medical insurance premiums and medical care	185,330	1.10
Exclusion of net imputed rental income	72,440	0.43
Deductibility of mortgage interest for owner-occupied homes	69,020	0.41
Tax treatment of capital gains (except agriculture, timber, iron ore, and coal)	68,860	0.41
Net exclusion of pension contributions and earnings to 401(k) plans	50,670	0.30
Deductibility of nonbusiness state and local taxes other than on owner-occupied homes	44,020	0.26
Deductibility of charitable contributions, other than education and health	39,620	0.23
Net exclusion of pension earnings and contributions to employer plans	37,860	0.23
Capital gains exclusion on home sales	34,270	0.20
Exclusion of interest on public-purpose state and local bonds	28,440	0.17
Total of top 10 individual tax expenditures	630,170	3.75

Source: Office of Management and Budget, *Fiscal Year 2015: Analytical Perspectives—Budget of the United States Government* (Washington, DC: Government Printing Office).

rate of $2,000 per month while paying the $1,500 monthly mortgage payment. The homeowner would then be consuming $2,000 of house per month but paying only $1,500—a difference of $500, which could be "imputed" as income to the homeowner. The tax expenditure "exclusion of imputed rental income" attempts to measure such income. It is easy to see why many people do not consider such amounts to be income in the traditional sense, because the "income" is imputed and not based on real money receipts.[22]

EQUITY

One defining characteristic of tax expenditures in the US income tax system is the propagation of vertical or horizontal inequities among taxpayers. Owing to the progressive nature of the income tax system, equity is generally concerned with concepts of fairness: whether taxpayers with similar incomes pay similar tax amounts and whether higher-income taxpayers pay proportionately more than those with lower incomes. The former is considered horizontal equity, and the latter vertical equity. For example, if two taxpayers have exactly the same income but one owns a home and deducts mortgage interest payments and the other rents, the taxpayer taking advantage of the mortgage interest deduction will likely pay less in income taxes than the person who rents. This situation could be viewed as a violation of horizontal equity. Additionally, the taxpayer with the mortgage deduction could earn more in income than the renter but still pay less in income taxes because of the mortgage interest deduction. In this case, there would be vertical inequity because the taxpayer who earns more is paying less in income tax. We next examine the successes and failures of equity promotion in the aftermath of TRA86 and then examine equity in the federal tax code.

Congress considered both horizontal and vertical equity while drafting TRA86, although TRA86's adjustment in vertical equity appeared to be a consequence of other primary concerns that drove tax reform. A 2004 study by Wenli Li and Pierre-Daniel Sarte finds that TRA86 decreased progressivity in the United States.[23] Horizontal equity was one of the centerpiece concerns of the act because individuals with equal incomes were often paying different tax amounts. Citing President Ronald Reagan's tax reform proposal (the recommendation was called Treasury II), tax economists Alan Auerbach and Joel Slemrod viewed horizontal equity as a driving political concern:

> "[People] can't understand the logic or equity of people in seemingly similar situations paying dramatically different amounts of tax." The President's proposal was promoted as "[reducing] the number of economically healthy income-earning individuals and corporations who . . . escape taxation altogether."[24]

Although many economists believed TRA86 promoted greater horizontal equity, the public did not agree. In polls conducted in 1986 and 1990, Gallup asked if TRA86 made for a "more fair," "less fair," or

Table 2.2. Gallup Polling Question Results, 1986 and 1990: Fairer Distribution of Tax Load

Question: "Do you think the Tax Reform Act of 1986 has made for a fairer distribution of the tax load among all taxpayers, one that's less fair, or is it not much different from the previous system?"

| | SHARE OF RESPONDENTS (%) | | | |
YEAR	FAIRER	NOT MUCH DIFFERENT	LESS FAIR	NO OPINION
1986	27	36	20	17
1990	9	40	37	14

Source: Gallup, *The Gallup Poll Monthly*, March 1990, 6–8.

"same" distribution of the tax load among all taxpayers. Within only four years, the share of taxpayers answering "more fair" fell from 27 percent to 9 percent, and the share of taxpayers answering "less fair" rose from 20 percent to 37 percent (see table 2.2).

Why did TRA86 fall short of the public's expectations? Progressivity had not decreased substantially, and taxpayers with similar incomes were paying more equal amounts. The problem was with a few significant inequities that were untouched by reform. Polling suggests that the public realized that TRA86 had not dealt with fundamental horizontal inequities or even intergenerational inequity. These inequities continue today and are often a focus of tax reform debates.

The first inequity was that employer-provided benefits remained untaxed under TRA86. Employees of a business that provided health care or pension benefits were likely taxed less than other taxpayers consuming a similar bundle of goods that was not provided by their employer. Today, businesses may still claim deductions for providing employee health care and pension benefits, rather than subjecting those expenditures to income and payroll taxes. Consequently, there is a roughly 30 percent price difference between employer-provided health insurance premiums and individual premiums.[25] The tax code's subsidization of employer-provided health care benefits not only creates different tax liabilities for individuals with otherwise equal incomes but also contributes to higher health care costs across the economy as a result of an overinvestment in tax-deductible benefits.[26] According to an article in the *Journal of the American Medical Association*, "Tax financing now covers more than 60 percent of U.S. health care costs."[27]

The second inequity pertains to elimination of the consumer interest deduction—for example, interest on credit card debt—without elimination of the mortgage interest deduction. By eliminating only one deduction, renters and homeowners—all else being equal—are treated differently. Holtz-Eakin describes the conflict as follows:

> Because consumer interest is no longer deductible, but mortgage interest remains deductible, homeowners have an incentive to borrow against their homes to purchase durable goods. The effect is to subsidize the interest costs of homeowners, but offer no equal subsidy to those individuals who rent.[28]

Although TRA86 eliminated many of the exemptions that generated inequity, the remaining tax expenditures became accentuated as inequities in the tax code. The most politically vulnerable tax deductions were eliminated, but the deductions with some of the greatest political support and economic cost—exclusion of employer-provided medical benefits and the mortgage interest deduction—were retained. President Obama's budget for fiscal year 2015 projected that these two provisions alone will decrease federal revenue between 2015 and 2019 by $1.15 trillion and $456 billion, respectively.[29] A 2009 study by the Urban Institute–Brookings Institution Tax Policy Center study estimates that owner-occupied housing, medical care, and retirement savings—as subsidized by existing tax expenditures—represent 47 percent of all tax expenditures, an incredible 3 percent of GDP.[30]

The third inequity not addressed by TRA86 was intergenerational equity. A strong reason TRA86 was able to become law was that it was revenue neutral, meaning it neither added to nor subtracted from the deficit. As Auerbach and Slemrod note, "The debate about tax reform proceeded separately from the discussion of what, if anything, to do about the large deficits of the time."[31] The five-year scoring focus on tax reform in the 1980s centered on equity concerns for current taxpayers, but it did not account for the future taxpayers who would be responsible for paying off the interest payments and debt of accelerated government spending. Although the federal tax code focuses on the financial interests of current taxpayers, individuals have a vested interest in the financial well-being of their children and grandchildren and the economic future their descendants will inherit. A tax break today without an offsetting spending cut may be seen as a future tax increase.[32] This economic future includes the national debt, which was caused in part by federal tax expenditures. To avoid repeating the mistakes of the past, future tax reform should be accompanied by substantial consideration of national debt reduction.

Eliminating tax expenditures will push some taxpayers into higher marginal tax brackets. Hence, equity concerns about eliminating tax expenditures are vital when considering the rate reductions that would likely accompany tax reform. As Chapoton testified, "If all tax expenditures were suddenly removed from the law, there could be a 34 percent reduction in tax rates across the board."[33] An across-the-board reduction would not lead to the same distribution of the tax burden following such a reform, though. To maintain the vertical equity of the present progressive tax system, all tax rates should be reduced by the same number of percentage points rather than by the same percentage, because high-income taxpayers benefit disproportionately from tax expenditures. Economists Leonard Burman, Christopher Geissler, and Eric Toder find that "eliminating tax expenditures would reduce after-tax income by 11.4 percent in the top quintile, 6.5 percent in the bottom quintile, and 9.6 percent on average for all income groups."[34]

But measuring the progressivity of tax expenditures may be inappropriate. Although tax expenditures benefit high-income taxpayers more in absolute terms and relative to income, low-income taxpayers benefit more relative to taxes paid.[35] Burman, Geissler, and Toder write:

> With all tax rates reduced by the same percentage, the substitution of rate reductions for tax expenditures would, on average, help high-income taxpayers and hurt lower-income taxpayers. With all tax rates reduced by the same *percentage points,* the substitution of rate reductions for tax expenditures would, on average, help low-income taxpayers and hurt high-income taxpayers.[36]

An increase or decrease of vertical equity will depend on the rate reductions that would likely accompany tax expenditure elimination.

SIMPLICITY

The US tax code increases in complexity as the number and use of tax expenditures and tax preferences increase. The financial goal of simplicity is to reduce compliance costs, whether those costs are incurred in the process of filing income tax returns or in complying with various tax laws on a day-to-day basis. TRA86 set this goal by reducing the number of individuals who would itemize deductions and who would be subject to the alternative minimum tax (AMT). A significant reduction in itemized filings would potentially reduce the overall compliance costs of the tax system (estimated to be between $215 billion and $987 billion annually, as noted in chapter 1). In addition, part of the simplicity generated by TRA86 was in going from 15 marginal tax brackets to only three. Even for taxpayers who itemize, TRA86 was meant to reduce the complexity of filing and the economic costs of personal time and professional tax assistance. We next examine what TRA86's achievements are purported to be, how the reforms failed to accomplish their intended goals, and how TRA86 failed to prevent an even more complicated tax code today.

Turning around the concept of complexity from the previous paragraph, we can illustrate the simplicity of a tax code by considering how many tax expenditure provisions are present and the extent to which those expenditures are used. Holtz-Eakin claims that three significant aspects reduced taxpayer compliance costs under TRA86: (a) the combined increase in personal exemptions and standard deductions, which reduced the number of filers who itemize; (b) the equalization of capital gains with ordinary income, which reduced portfolio planning; and (c) the combination of increased deductions and exemptions with a lower tax rate, which discouraged tax evasion.[37]

In terms of calculating the number of tax filers who itemize deductions, Holtz-Eakin is correct. By increasing the standard deduction and lowering tax rates, TRA86 reduced the percentage of taxpayers who itemize from 39.47 in 1986 to 28.44 in 1989. Additionally, the number of tax filers who were subject to the complicated AMT fell from 608,906 in 1986 to 101,176 in 1989.[38] However, despite the decrease in the number of tax filers who itemized deductions, tax returns with a paid preparer's signature increased slightly to 47.03 percent in 1989 from 46.63 percent in 1986.[39] This finding suggests that tax expenditure elimination was not substantial enough to decrease the need for professional preparer assistance. A 1992 survey by Marsha Blumenthal and Joel Slemrod finds that the average amount of time households spent preparing tax returns between 1982 and 1989 increased from 21.7 hours to 27.4 hours and that average expenditures for professional tax assistance increased from $42 to $66.[40] These numbers offer a compelling case against the notion that compliance costs decreased under TRA86 even though the federal tax code had been made simpler. Holtz-Eakin remarks that eliminating some expenditures—such as income averaging—has had little effect on compliance costs, saying that "simpler does not necessarily mean better."[41] In other words, as long as substantial tax expenditures exist that encourage professional tax planning, compliance costs may be expected to remain high.

In the 1990 Gallup poll referenced earlier, respondents were asked whether TRA86 had made tax filing "less complicated," "more complicated," or "the same." Within only four years, the share of taxpayers who answered "less complicated" had fallen from 19 percent to 12 percent, and the share of taxpayers who said "more complicated" had risen from 17 percent to 31 percent (see table 2.3). On one hand, the results are surprising considering the decrease in the number of filers who itemized deductions. On the other

Table 2.3. Gallup Polling Question Results, 1986 and 1990: Complexity of Tax Code

Question: "Do you think the Tax Reform Act of 1986 has made it less complicated for you to pay your taxes, more complicated, or about the same as the previous system?"

	SHARE OF RESPONDENTS (%)			
		ABOUT		
	LESS	THE	MORE	NO
YEAR	COMPLICATED	SAME	COMPLICATED	OPINION
1986	19	51	17	13
1990	12	48	31	9

Source: Gallup, *The Gallup Poll Monthly*, March 1990, 6–8.

hand, perhaps the results are not surprising given the increased spending on professional tax assistance after TRA86's enactment.

Slemrod concludes in his study that the available evidence suggests TRA86 did little to prevent the rising compliance costs of the individual income tax system.[42] Why? The likely answer is that although TRA86 eliminated many tax expenditures, the biggest and most frequently used expenditures went untouched. As shown in figure 2.1, the number of tax expenditures has increased since passage of TRA86.[43] And as other tax expenditures were eliminated, taxpayers looking to reduce their tax liabilities invested in the remaining deductions with more resources.

According to the Congressional Research Service, "[T]ax expenditures experienced a large decline relative to GDP between 1987 and 1989 largely because of the effects of the Tax Reform Act of 1986, which

Figure 2.1. Number of Tax Expenditures, 1975–2013

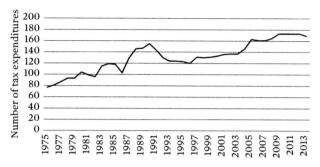

Source: Data from the budgets of the US government, fiscal years 1977–2013.

broadened the tax base by eliminating several tax expenditures and reduced tax rates."[44] Shortly before passage of TRA86, tax expenditures were estimated to be slightly below 10 percent of GDP, and they declined to under 6 percent by 1989. Since then, total tax expenditures rose slowly to just below 8 percent of GDP by 2008.[45]

For tax reform today to reduce compliance costs, all tax expenditures must be on the table, including the highly protected mortgage interest deduction and the exemption for employer-provided benefits. The arrival to today's labyrinth of a tax code began with the Omnibus Budget Reconciliation Act of 1990 and the Omnibus Budget Reconciliation Act of 1993. The achievements of TRA86 in reducing itemized deductions unraveled quickly, and 14,000 additional changes to federal tax law had occurred by 2005.[46] The Joint Committee on Taxation notes that tax expenditures in 2012 totaled $1.2 trillion—87 percent for individual tax returns and 13 percent ($155 billion) for corporate tax returns.[47] Corporate tax expenditures remained far from insignificant—roughly 64 percent of 2012 corporate tax receipts ($242 billion).[48]

One unexpected lesson from TRA86 is that most tax expenditures eliminated by the law have not returned. Perhaps they have been deemed bad policy or have become politically untouchable. Passive loss exemption (except on housing), the personal consumer interest deduction, income averaging, and restrictions on miscellaneous businesses expenses have not been reinstated. State and local income tax deductions were reinstated in 2004, and the two-earner deduction was added back by the Economic Growth and Tax Relief Reconciliation Act of 2001.

The increase in federal tax expenditures (see figure 2.1) since TRA86 suggests that the political system gravitates toward special interests and is actually innovative in aiding them. Today, the United States continues to have a federal tax code that is riddled with both new exemptions and many tax expenditure fortresses similar to those that existed before TRA86. The economic size of these tax expenditures continues to grow, although the total size relative to GDP is relatively constant (see figure 2.2).[49]

The revenue raised by eliminating these tax expenditures, however, could be even higher than the projected forgone revenue. Burman, Geissler, and Toder claim that eliminating a large share of nonbusiness individual income tax expenditures would raise about 8 percent more revenue than the sum of individual estimates for each provision:

The interaction effects are largest for itemized deductions, and reduce instead of increase the combined effect of the separate provisions because, when an itemized deduction is eliminated, taxpayers who are not on the AMT are more likely to take the standard deduction. For example, if the mortgage interest deduction were eliminated, millions fewer taxpayers would itemize deductions and thus would get no benefit from deducting charitable contributions.[50]

Numerous new tax expenditures have increased the complexity of the US tax code and necessitated higher tax rates to achieve certain revenue targets, all else being equal. Tax expenditures have become so prevalent that John Chapoton, former assistant secretary of the treasury, testified that a 34 percent across-the-board reduction in tax rates would result if all tax expenditures were removed.[51]

Figure 2.2. Size of Tax Expenditures, 1975–2013

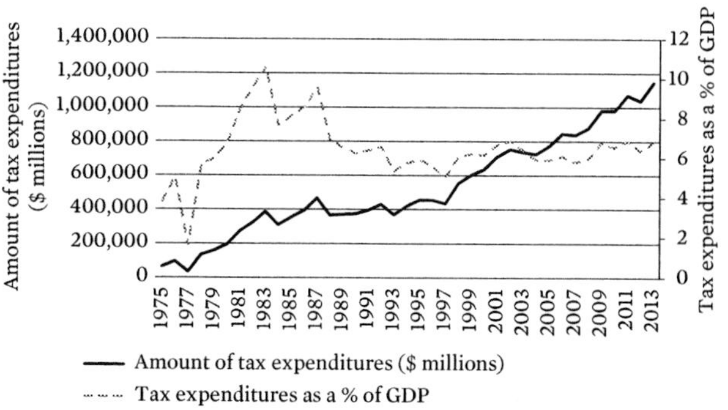

—— Amount of tax expenditures ($ millions)
- - - - Tax expenditures as a % of GDP

PUBLIC CHOICE COSTS OF THE
INCOME TAX SYSTEM

In addition to the compliance and efficiency costs incurred because of the federal tax code, lobbyists and special-interest groups expend great resources (time, money, and so forth) in an attempt to gain or preserve tax preferences. These lobbying expenditures are known as *rent-seeking costs*.[52] The concept of rent-seeking costs emerged from the field of public choice theory, largely developed from the work of Nobel laureate James Buchanan and colleague Gordon Tullock. Such rent-seeking costs are objectionable because these resources carry opportunity costs of productive processes. Economist Randall Holcombe took the ideas of Buchanan and applied them to the tax policy process. He wrote that the easier it is to modify a tax system, the greater the incentive for special interests to pursue rent-seeking behavior. Once tax expenditures are successfully obtained, additional rent-seeking expenditures are incurred to keep those deductions in place.[53]

Tax specialist James Poterba poses a solution to the lobbying expenditure problem with a simple, stable, and broad tax system: "In this framework, proportional income taxation, or sales taxes levied at the same rate on all goods, would reduce the opportunity for lobbying."[54] Holcombe conjectures that adopting a broad-based retail tax or value-added tax (VAT) might reduce political expenditures.[55] Although this chapter does not advocate for a national retail sales tax or VAT, such a reform could plausibly maintain a broad tax base more easily than the income tax system.

As Slemrod states, "[The] stability of the tax system is an important element of simplicity."[56] The temporary nature of many tax expenditures carries an opportunity cost because of uncertainty. Uncertainty potentially restricts the investment decisions of taxpayers and businesses and has the potential to inhibit economic growth.[57] Public choice theory predicts that greater uncertainty over the tax code translates into higher rent-seeking expenditures.

THE 2 PERCENT TAX EXPENDITURE SOLUTION

One tax expenditure reform, proposed by Martin Feldstein, Daniel Feenberg, and Maya MacGuineas, would cap the use of tax expenditures at 2 percent of aggregate income. These authors claim that such a reform would reduce the number of itemized filers from 48 million to 13 million (a decrease of 75 percent) and would have reduced the fiscal year 2011 deficit by $278 billion dollars, or about 1.8 percent of projected GDP.[58]

Additionally, restricting the use of tax expenditures prevents some tax evasion and maintains a broad tax base. Although Feldstein, Feenberg, and MacGuineas's reform is progressive in absolute terms, it is regressive in terms of taxes paid as a percentage of income for low-income taxpayers. For example, individuals with an aggregate income up to $25,000 would be taxed 3.6 percent more under the 2 percent cap, whereas individuals making over $500,000 would pay only

2.7 percent more in taxes.[59] However, the 2 percent cap would not necessarily be progressive depending on how rate cuts were enacted, assuming that a cut in standard tax rates accompanied such a reform.[60]

Kleinbard agrees that some type of mechanism is needed to rein in uncapped tax expenditures. He is skeptical, though, about using a cap to limit tax expenditures instead of forcing "a substantive renegotiation of the present tax system."[61] Instead, he believes that Congress will revisit tax expenditures "as a substantive matter when [it] decides it is hungry enough for the revenue or for a more efficient tax system."[62] For Kleinbard, successful tax reform must be centered on cleaning up the tax code rather than restraining a tax code littered with special interests. Although a 2 percent solution may have a lasting effect by reducing the number of filed claims, success in terms of efficiency and equity may be short lived. Following TRA86, the innovative approach of special-interest groups to reassemble the federal tax code to their liking suggests that policy successes may be short lived as long as the tax code remains so easily manipulated. Moreover, Congress would still be able to increase a cap for tax expenditures or even complicate the tax code further by exempting certain deductions from the cap.

LESSONS FROM TRA86 REGARDING PRESENT-DAY TAX EXPENDITURES

Holtz-Eakin states that one major political statement of TRA86 was to reaffirm annual income as the fundamental basis for taxation in the United States for the foreseeable future.[63] This is the beginning point that tax reform needs to address. Despite TRA86's bipartisan support to broaden the tax base and lower tax rates, tax expenditures returned quickly to the tax code and in even greater numbers.

In a Tax Foundation publication, Gerald Prante summarizes the two deepest flaws of TRA86 as follows:

> While the legislation did close special tax shelters for select individuals—events that often became nightly news stories—the reform did little to close the many significant exemptions that inhibit overall economic growth. Also, much of what passed in 1986 to limit special tax loopholes has already crept back into the system courtesy of politicians quick to give in to whatever lobby fills their pockets.[64]

In an increasingly competitive global economy, federal spending can no longer be financed by using the easy-to-manipulate and complex income tax system. The United States needs a stable, simple tax system with a broad base and low rates to finance federal spending and increase global business competitiveness.[65] The federal government needs to examine the potential benefits of completely replacing the income tax system with a broad-based consumption tax. Again, although this chapter does not advocate for a national retail sales tax or VAT, especially combined with income taxes, it is necessary to point out that a consumption tax might promote efficiency and equity, which TRA86 failed to do. Such a tax system would address the costly and economically inefficient employer-provided benefits exemptions and mortgage interest deduction by eliminating these inequities from the federal tax code. Broadening the tax base would not only increase the efficiency of resource distribution but would also be "key to dealing with the perception of unfairness."[66]

A broad-based consumption tax could also restrict opportunities for rent-seeking behavior. A stable and broad tax system could have a lasting effect on decreasing compliance costs and rent-seeking behavior because lobbyists and special-interest groups would have fewer opportunities to riddle the tax code with exemptions and deductions. Michael Graetz identifies one of the inherent weaknesses of TRA86 as its being "based on retaining and strengthening the income tax, rather than heeding the calls of many economists and politicians to replace it with some form of consumption tax."[67] Charles McClure Jr. and George Zodrow state that the Treasury plan "showed conclusively just how complex a relatively pure income tax can be, [and that] the Tax Reform Act of 1986 makes strikingly clear that a tax that is less pure is sure to be even more complicated."[68] Even a tax system that allows for only a few substantial tax expenditures keeps the door open for high annual compliance costs as taxpayers continue to seek professional assistance to reduce their tax liabilities.

Successful reform of the US tax code must be based on lessons learned from TRA86—both its accomplishments and its failures. Against an array of special-interest groups, the bipartisan reform that occurred with passage of the act promoted greater efficiency, equity, and simplicity in the tax code. The problem is that TRA86 did not establish a principle of opposing tax preferences in general by failing to tear down the largest tax expenditures, which have since continued to grow. In exchange for lowering tax rates, even those tax expenditures that are considered politically untouchable must now be on the table if the tax code is to be fundamentally reformed to promote strong and stable economic growth. Additionally, it might be necessary to create institutional reforms to prevent future tax expenditures from being added later. Failure to learn from the lessons of TRA86 will only doom future reform efforts.

CHAPTER 3
Why Should Congress Restructure the Corporate Income Tax?

To increase employment and expand their economies, most developed countries are moving toward reducing their corporate income tax rates and restructuring their corporate income tax systems. The United States appears to be taking the opposite approach. Consequently, the increasingly burdensome US corporate income tax structure is driving competitive, profit-seeking American corporations to minimize their tax exposure and defer income overseas to countries with lower tax rates. Unless the United States reforms its corporate income tax system, the country will continue to fall further behind in global competitiveness.

US political leaders are well aware of this problem. In his 2011 State of the Union Address, President Barack Obama said the following:

> Over the years, a parade of lobbyists has rigged the tax code to benefit particular companies and industries. Those with accountants or lawyers to work the system can end up paying no taxes at

This chapter was adapted from a paper written by Jason J. Fichtner and Nicholas J. Tuszynski.

all. But all the rest are hit with one of the highest corporate tax rates in the world. It makes no sense, and it has to change. . . . So tonight, I'm asking Democrats and Republicans to simplify the system. Get rid of the loopholes. Level the playing field. And use the savings to lower the corporate tax rate for the first time in 25 years—without adding to our deficit.[1]

Speaking to National Public Radio in 2011, then–House Budget Committee Chairman Paul Ryan (R-WI), who is now chairman of the House Ways and Means Committee, agreed that the existing corporate tax system is stifling America's long-term fiscal goals: "We are beginning to get a consensus that this corporate tax system we have is very uncompetitive. It pushes jobs overseas. It locks capital up overseas."[2]

President Obama and Chairman Ryan are correct. If Congress does not overhaul the corporate income tax structure, the United States will continue to lose jobs to countries with lower taxes, domestic firms will become increasingly less competitive internationally, and investment in the United States will continue to decline. This chapter begins by looking at the US corporate income tax rate and the corporate tax system and compares those of the United States with those of other countries. The chapter then examines problems with the current US system and shows how these problems hinder the long-term economic growth of the country.

HOW CORPORATE INCOME TAX RATES WORK

What does *corporate income tax rate* mean? Political pundits and the news media use the term frequently but rarely explain it. Furthermore, the corporate income tax rate can be defined in many ways. To compare countries and empirical information, one must use the appropriate definition. The corporate income tax rate in fact consists of three different rates that must be examined together:

- *National statutory rate.* This rate is the central government's tax rate, imposed by law, that is assessed on corporate profits. Like individual income tax rates, corporate income tax rates are progressive, increasing with higher levels of income. Discussions of statutory rates typically refer to the top marginal rate. In the United States, corporations that earn profits of more than $18.3 million are taxed at the top marginal rate of 35 percent.

- *Statutory combined rate.* The statutory combined rate is the central government's statutory rate plus state and local tax rates. The United States has a top corporate tax rate of 35 percent; along with the average combined state and local rate of 4.1 percent, the total statutory rate for corporations is 39.1 percent. However, corporations rarely pay the highest rate because of tax preferences, so focusing solely on statutory rates can be misleading.

Table 3.1. US and OECD Corporate Income Tax Rates, 2013

TYPE OF RATE	UNITED STATES (%)	OECD AVERAGE (%)	US RANK
National statutory rate	35.0	23.3	34th out of 34
Statutory combined rate	39.1	25.5	33rd out of 34

Source: PricewaterhouseCoopers, "Assessing Tax: 2013 Tax Rate Benchmarking Study for Industrial Products and Automotive Products," May 2013; OECD, "Taxation of Corporate and Capital Income," table II.I, Paris, May 2013; KPMG, "Corporate Tax Rates Table," http://www.kpmg.com/global/en/services/tax/tax-tools-and-resources/pages/corporate-tax-rates-table.aspx.

- *Effective tax rate.* The effective tax rate is the amount of income tax divided by total corporate income. The rate accounts for all deductions, credits, depreciation, and preferences in the tax code and yields the percentage of income that a corporation actually pays in taxes.

Table 3.1 shows where the United States ranks among developed countries in terms of the national statutory and statutory combined tax rates. Because of preferences in the tax code, effective tax rates vary widely from industry to industry. See the appendix for trends in the effective tax rates applying to different industries.

As a baseline for comparison, table 3.1 shows the average corporate tax rate for member countries of the Organisation for Economic Co-operation and Development (OECD). The average national statu-

Figure 3.1. National Statutory Corporate Income Tax Rates in OECD Countries, 2013

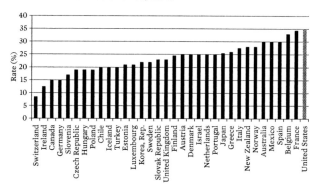

Source: OECD, "Taxation of Corporate and Capital Income," table II.I, Paris, May 2013.

tory rate for the OECD countries is 23 percent, and the average statutory combined rate is 25 percent. As of 2013, the United States had the highest statutory rate in the developed world and was second worldwide to the United Arab Emirates.[3] Uncompetitive US corporate tax rates, combined with the advantages of today's advanced communication technologies, lead certain US corporations to invest in other developed countries that have lower tax rates.[4] This situation threatens the health of the US economy. Figure 3.1 shows how the United States ranks compared to other OECD countries.

The gap between the US corporate tax rate and the rates of other developed countries was not always so large. In 1990, the OECD member countries' average statutory combined rate was 41.1 percent and the US rate was 38.7 percent. But less than a decade later,

Figure 3.2. Average Statutory Combined Corporate Income Tax Rates, 1990–2012

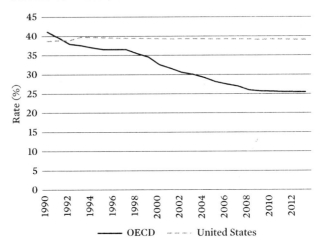

Source: OECD, "Taxation of Corporate and Capital Income," table II.I, Paris, May 2013.

in 1999, the average statutory combined rate for the OECD countries had fallen to 34.8 percent, as countries tried to either arrest capital flight or attract capital inflow. The US statutory combined rate, however, had risen to 39.4 percent by then. Overall, the OECD rates have continued to fall, but US rates have remained high. Figure 3.2 illustrates the widening gap from 1990 through 2012.

Over a 20-year period, developed countries such as Germany, Sweden, and Hungary cut their corporate tax rates by 20 percentage points (see figure 3.3).[5] These countries have different economic and political institutions, yet they have all broken

Figure 3.3. Statutory Combined Corporate Tax Rate Cuts in Selected Countries, 1990–2013

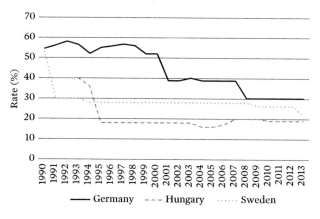

Source: OECD, "Taxation of Corporate and Capital Income," table II.I, Paris, May 2013; Jason J. Fichtner and Nick Tuszynski, "Why the United States Needs to Restructure the Corporate Income Tax," Mercatus Working Paper 11-42, Mercatus Center at George Mason University, Arlington, VA, November 2011.

through barriers to decrease their corporate income tax rates.

A focus on only the US statutory corporate income tax rate could misrepresent the rate that corporations actually pay. The statutory rate is a ceiling. As explained previously, the effective tax rate, which accounts for all deductions, credits, depreciation, and tax code preferences, reflects what corporations actually pay in income taxes. Between 1994 and 2010, the effective tax rate for US corporations ranged between 21.8 and 27.8 percent. This range is higher than the OECD average and places the United States as having one of the highest rates in the world.

WORLDWIDE VS. TERRITORIAL TAX SYSTEMS

Another important aspect of the corporate income tax system is the way in which taxes are allocated and collected. There are two basic types of international tax systems: worldwide and territorial.[6] The US system is basically a worldwide system whereby businesses registered as US domestic companies are subject to taxation on all income regardless of whether the income is earned domestically or internationally. The US government taxes profits generated by certain types of overseas activities in the year the profits are earned, but it does not tax profits from other activities until the corporation repatriates that income to the United States. Domestic corporations may take a credit for taxes paid on foreign income to foreign tax authorities, up to the US tax rate, so that the business is not taxed by both a foreign tax authority and the United States on the same income. However, complex rules limit US corporations from taking full credit for foreign taxes. If a foreign tax rate is less than 35 percent, as it is in all other OECD countries, US corporations have a tax incentive to keep their profits overseas.

The United States is one of the few countries in the developed world that still uses a worldwide-based corporate income tax system. Many foreign corporations that trade with the United States are incorporated in countries that operate under a territorial tax system. As of 2012, 28 OECD member countries had implemented a territorial tax system, whereas only 6 continued to use a worldwide tax system.[7] The other five OECD countries operating under a worldwide system had a 2013 average statutory corporate income tax rate of 22.3 percent, which is much lower than the 35 percent rate the United States imposes. In essence, the current US corporate tax system is a tax on exports and can be viewed as imposing double taxation on overseas profits, which hinders this country's ability to compete economically with other nations.

The tax treatment of corporate income from foreign-owned corporations creates a tax disadvantage for domestically owned corporations. Consider just one illustrative example. Until TRA86, foreign shipping income earned by US controlled foreign corporations was eligible for deferral treatment. It was reinstated with the American Jobs Creation Act of 2004. But as the Department of Treasury points out in a 2002 paper,

> No country has rules for the immediate taxation of foreign-source income that are comparable to the U.S. rules in terms of breadth and complexity. For example, the U.S. tax system imposes current tax on the income earned by a U.S.-owned foreign subsidiary from its shipping operations, while that company's foreign-owned competitors are not subject to tax on their shipping income. Consequently, the U.S.-based company's margin on such operations is reduced by the amount of the tax, putting it at a disadvantage relative to the foreign competitor that does not bear such a tax. The U.S.-based company has less income to reinvest in its business, which can mean less growth and reduced future opportunities for that company.[8]

The complicated US corporate income tax system could be greatly simplified, and the playing field with trading partners leveled, if the United States moved toward a territorial system. Potential reforms include exempting all foreign-source income, exempting only active foreign-source income, or exempting only certain kinds of foreign-source income.[9] Such reforms would significantly reduce the inefficiencies, inequities, and complexities of the current US corporate tax system and would produce substantial economic benefits. Furthermore, adopting a territorial tax system would remove a major incentive that exists now for US multinational corporations to move their headquarters operations overseas. Both Japan and the United Kingdom adopted territorial tax systems in 2009 to compete with other markets and expand their economies.[10]

A territorial system has numerous advantages over the more complicated worldwide tax system. It allows corporations to focus less on complex accounting strategies and concentrate more on growth, investment, and production. A less complicated corporate income tax system with territorial principles would also mean less red tape within the US tax code, allowing for less bureaucracy to administer and enforce tax laws.

THE PERILS OF A HIGH CORPORATE TAX RATE

Corporations respond to high tax rates by relocating their economic activity to lower-tax countries. The current US corporate tax structure puts

US-headquartered corporations at a tremendous disadvantage in the global marketplace because other countries have lowered their corporate income tax rates to welcome multinational corporations. In December 2010, then–Prime Minister Naoto Kan said he hoped to stimulate Japan's slow economy with a corporate tax rate cut of 5 percentage points.[11] The United Kingdom underwent a multiyear process to lower its combined corporate tax rate to 20 percent by 2015.[12]

Canada lowered its national corporate tax rate from 18 percent to 16.5 percent in 2011 and further to 15 percent in 2012, giving it a combined rate of roughly 26 percent once the provincial tax rate is included.[13] Canada had good reason to lower its rate. A 2011 study by Duanjie Chen and Jack Mintz, of the University of Calgary, estimates that a 3 percent reduction in Canada's national statutory rate, from 18 percent to 15 percent, would create 100,000 jobs and draw $30 billion in additional business investment over a seven-year period.[14] An independent study by Canadian Manufacturers & Exporters finds that a similar rate cut would create 98,000 jobs in a two-year period.[15]

The corporate income tax rate plays a major role in determining where a corporation will invest capital.[16] Thanks to today's communication technologies, corporations that do business together often do not require physical proximity. Thus, if two countries are similar in culture, infrastructure, and economic growth potential and one has a dramatically lower corporate income tax rate than the other, it would be financially irresponsible for an entrepreneur or an expanding corporation to invest in the country with the higher rate.

US corporations have been and are continuing to move outside the United States to initiate and expand business opportunities. Their share of worldwide profits attributable to foreign revenue increased from 6.7 percent in 1965 to 38.2 percent in 2009.[17] Not only do such investment shifts create losses and impede growth for corporations; they also create losses for American workers because corporations choose not to use profits to create more jobs in this country.

DISTORTED INCENTIVES

With a US corporate income tax rate that is so much higher than in other countries, American corporations must turn their accounting departments into profit-maximizing centers. Corporations need complex financial engineering tactics to minimize revenue losses using existing tax code preferences. Through various transfer-pricing arrangements, accountants can allot income and capital to different countries to minimize tax liabilities and help corporations remain competitive.

Many corporations spend more time and resources using tax rules as profit centers than they do focusing on potential business investment. This system is inefficient because the resources used to combat the corporate income tax could be invested in intellectual or physical capital. Investment could help a corporation grow, which would lead to more jobs and output and would expand the domestic economy. Instead, the high US corporate income tax rate distorts the incentive structures and investment behaviors of corporations. It is sometimes more "profitable" for corporations to invest in lobbyists who can work to expand tax preferences than to use their financial resources to expand business output.[18] Federal tax policy should instead provide the proper structure to encourage business growth. The current US corporate tax structure forces American businesses to misallocate resources, causing a ripple effect throughout the financial structure of corporations. The high US corporate tax rate means that corporations must cut costs or raise prices elsewhere to compete with businesses based in countries with lower corporate income tax rates.

Recently, both job creation and economic growth have been key topics among economic policy advisors. Restructuring the US corporate tax system would address both issues. Policymakers debate the need for the federal government to continue investing in economic growth, yet such investment can do little good when current economic policies actually inhibit growth. When other countries have lower corporate income tax rates, corporations may choose overseas destinations for business. Estimates of how many domestic jobs the current corporate income tax has quashed range from 200,000 to 3 million,[19] but the consensus is that many employees are laid off specifically because of the high costs imposed by the current US corporate tax structure. During the 2000s, major multinational corporations have reduced US jobs by

2.9 million while increasing overseas employment by 2.4 million.[20] Not all of these jobs were cut and outsourced specifically because of the US corporate tax system. But was the system a contributing factor? Absolutely. Although outsourcing is no longer popular, it remains an option for almost any multinational corporation seeking to reduce costs, including costs imposed by the corporate income tax.

BURDEN OF TAX FALLS ON INDIVIDUALS

A tax on a corporation is an additional tax on individuals. Many people view corporations as faceless entities whose tax burden is unimportant. But corporations are made up of individual investors and workers attempting to earn money by maximizing profits. Corporations are not the only ones affected by corporate income tax rates. In addition to investors and workers, individual consumers are affected when high tax rates force corporations to charge more for their products and services. The highly flawed US corporate tax system is, thus, a form of double taxation on workers, consumers, and investors alike. Economist Steven Horwitz notes that the corporate income tax has "negative effects on real human beings" in several ways:

> If corporations respond by reducing compensation or firing workers, the impact of the tax hits the employees. If they raise prices, the impact falls on the consumers who buy the product. And if they take a reduction in profits, the falling stock

value lowers the value of various investment funds on which millions of Americans depend for retirement and other income. [21]

As a report of the Joint Economic Committee explains, "Any tax imposed on corporations results in either a reduction to employee wages, an increase in costs passed on to consumers, a reduction in the return to capital received by shareholders, or a combination of all three."[22] A working paper published by the Congressional Budget Office suggests that workers bear "slightly more than 70 percent of the burden of the corporate income tax."[23] Moreover, economists Kevin Hassett and Aparna Mathur find an interesting unseen consequence of raising tax rates. For every 1 percent increase in corporate tax rates, they find a 1 percent decrease in wages.[24] This finding illustrates that corporations respond to incentives and allocate resources within given constraints. Moreover, it indicates another way by which individuals ultimately bear the burden of any corporate tax.

DECREASED ECONOMIC GROWTH AND TAX REVENUE

The existing US corporate income tax also impedes the country's economic growth. A 2008 working paper published by the National Bureau of Economic Research on effective corporate tax rates concludes that a "10 percent increase in an effective tax rate reduces the aggregate investment to GDP ratio by 2 percentage points."[25] The paper also shows that high

Figure 3.4. US Statutory Corporate Income Tax Receipts as a Share of GDP

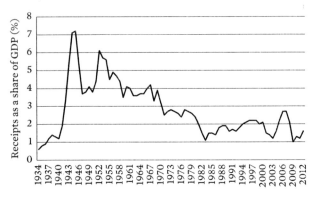

Source: Office of Management and Budget, "Receipts by Source as Percentages of GDP: 1934–2018," table 2.3, http://www.whitehouse.gov/sites/default/files/omb/budget/fy2014/assets/hist02z3.xls.

corporate tax rates are negatively correlated with economic growth.

A higher corporate tax rate may actually lead to less government revenue than a lower rate would. The high corporate tax rates give US corporations an incentive to keep their profits overseas so that they can defer paying taxes in the United States. Business news articles widely report that US corporations have $2.1 trillion in profits held overseas, which is estimated to reduce corporate tax revenue to the US Treasury by almost $50 billion in 2014.[26] Indeed, US corporate tax revenue is lower than that of many OECD countries, even as a percentage of GDP.[27] As figure 3.4 shows, even as the US economy has grown, corporate tax receipts as a percentage of GDP have decreased and have remained between 1 percent and 3 percent since 1990. A study by economists Alex Brill and Kevin Hassett shows significant evidence that lowering the US corporate tax rate would enhance tax revenue.[28]

CONCLUSION

The uncompetitive US corporate tax system impedes American corporations' ability to compete in the global marketplace. It also discourages potential domestic investment. If the United States is to be competitive in the future, federal corporate tax restructuring must occur. While other nations have been racing to slash corporate tax rates over the past 20 years, the United States has stagnated. At times the federal government has enacted temporary changes to corporate tax policy, but the fundamental problems that need permanent reform have been ignored.

The United States has an infamously dense and complicated tax code that is in dire need of simplification. Systemic problems exist not only with tax loopholes and havens but also with the uncompetitive high corporate income tax rate and the worldwide-based tax system, which together encourage American businesses to move jobs and investment overseas and to lobby for more loopholes. High corporate income taxes lead to lower wages and less investment and also hinder long-term economic growth at home. To protect American jobs and secure future fiscal stability for the country, the United States must slash its corporate tax rate to at least the OECD average, preferably below, and must move toward a territorial tax system. Absent sweeping corporate income tax reform, US competitiveness will continue to decline. Continued inaction by Congress will create troublesome results: the foreign outsourcing of economic activity, a further loss of American jobs, the sale of US businesses to foreign multinational corporations, a further erosion of the corporate tax base, and the continuation of harmful tax policies that are biased against saving, investment, job creation, and economic growth.

CHAPTER 4

Why Do Workers Bear a Significant Share of the Corporate Income Tax?

Who bears the cost of corporate taxation: the owners of capital or the workers?[1] Corporate income tax reform debates can become bogged down in whether corporations pay their "fair share" of taxes or whether the revenue effects of tax reform should be scored dynamically or calculated by using a static model. But debaters often overlook who ultimately bears the true costs of corporate income taxes.[2] Estimates of how the corporate income tax burden is divided between owners of capital and workers vary, from the Treasury Department's ratio of 82:18 to one frequently cited study's estimate of 30:70.[3] If one group has the opportunity to decrease its tax burden, there can be additional long-term costs and even deadweight losses from corporate income taxation. This chapter examines tax incidence in the long term—after corporations have had the opportunity to relocate capital across industries and to other countries.

Determining who bears the burden of corporate taxation can help policymakers understand the long-run behavioral responses of both workers and

Table 4.1. Five Drivers of Corporate Tax Incidence and Their Effects

DRIVER OF CORPORATE TAX INCIDENCE	SHARE OF TAX BURDEN FALLING ON CAPITAL GAINS	SHARE OF TAX BURDEN FALLING ON LABOR
High international product substitution	↓	↑
High GDP (size of country)	↑	↓
High international capital mobility	↓	↑
High factor substitution (labor for capital)[a]	↑	↓
High degree of industry capital intensity	↓	↑

Source: Jennifer Gravelle, "Corporate Tax Incidence: Review of General Equilibrium Estimates and Analysis," *National Tax Journal* 66, no. 1 (March 2013): 185–214. The order in which the five drivers appear in this chapter is different from the order used in Gravelle's submission to the *National Tax Journal.*
a. Jennifer Gravelle writes about labor substitution as follows: "The less firms can substitute for capital, the larger the burden that labor will bear."

businesses to the US corporate income tax code. If American companies are becoming more sensitive to US corporate income taxation, a migration of new or existing capital to foreign countries can be expected. This chapter does not provide elasticity estimates for capital; instead, it examines five different drivers laid out by Jennifer Gravelle, an economist with the Congressional Budget Office, that determine how sensitive capital is to corporate taxation in an open-economy framework. These drivers are (a) high international product substitution, (b) high GDP,

(c) high capital mobility, (d) high factor substitution, and (e) high degree of industry capital intensity (see table 4.1).[4] After examining the five drivers, we conclude that the sensitivity of US businesses to corporate taxation is increasing and that the amount of capital invested in the United States may further decrease in the long term as a result.

LITERATURE REVIEW OF CORPORATE INCOME TAX INCIDENCE

One of the most frequently cited studies on corporate income tax incidence is a 2006 paper by Jane Gravelle and Kent Smetters. These authors problematically give weight to short-run empirical estimates of imperfect product substitution and ignore the effect of corporate income tax on capital growth, both of which are key contributors to their conclusion that domestic labor's burden is only 21 percent of corporate tax revenue.[5] In her 2013 survey of the existing literature, Jennifer Gravelle estimates that 40 percent of the corporate tax burden falls on labor and 60 percent on capital—concluding that the United States operates in more of a closed economy than most models assume.[6] This chapter examines Jennifer Gravelle's five drivers of incidence and concludes that capital bears a decreasing share of the corporate income tax burden because the United States continues to become a more open economy. For example, increasing international capital mobility means that labor's share of the corporate income tax increases, whereas capital's share decreases, all other things being equal.

Table 4.2. Research Summaries on Corporate Income Tax Incidence

STUDY	EFFECT OF CORPORATE INCOME TAX ON WAGES	IMPORTANT DIFFERENCES IN SCOPE AND ASSUMPTIONS
Arulampalam, Devereux, and Maffini (2012)	Each $1 increase in the tax bill reduces median real wage by $0.49.	Measures effect of corporate income tax paid by firms on employee compensation using data on more than 500,000 firms in 9 European countries from 1996 to 2003
Felix and Hines (2009)	Each $1 increase in the tax bill reduces union wages by $0.54	Uses data from 2000 to estimate effects of state corporate income taxes on union wages
Hassett and Mathur (2010)	Each $1 increase in tax revenues leads to a $3 to $4 decrease in real wages.	Uses aggregate wage and tax data within the manufacturing sector for 72 countries from 1981 to 2002 in a general equilibrium model
Felix (2007)	A 1 percentage point increase in top statutory corporate income tax rate decreases annual wages by 0.7%.	Uses aggregate data on wages of workers at different skill levels from 19 Organisation for Economic Co-operation and Development countries over the period 1979–2000
Desai, Foley, and Hines (2007)	Labor bears between 45% and 75% of corporate income tax incidence.	Uses data from US multinational firms operating in 50 countries from 1989 to 2004 to jointly estimate the relative share of corporate income tax borne by labor and capital

Table 4.2. (*continued*)

STUDY	EFFECT OF CORPORATE INCOME TAX ON WAGES	IMPORTANT DIFFERENCES IN SCOPE AND ASSUMPTIONS
Liu and Altshuler (2013)	The burden of a $1 increase in the corporate income tax liability borne by labor is about $0.60	Uses data on individual US workers matched with industry-level effective marginal tax rates and industry concentration ratios in a general equilibrium model to analyze the extent to which imperfect competition affects the incidence of the corporate income tax

Sources: Wiji Arulampalam, Michael P. Devereux, and Giorgia Maffini, "The Direct Incidence of Corporate Income Tax on Wages," *European Economic Review* 56, no. 6 (August 2012): 1038–54; R. Alison Felix and James Hines, "Corporate Taxes and Union Wages in the United States," NBER Working Paper 15263, National Bureau of Economic Research, Cambridge, MA, 2009; Kevin A. Hassett and Aparna Mathur, "Spatial Tax Competition and Domestic Wages," Working Paper 185, American Enterprise Institute, Washington, DC, 2010; Alison R. Felix, "Passing the Burden: Corporate Tax Incidence in Open Economies," Regional Research Working Paper 07-01, Federal Reserve Bank of Kansas City, Kansas City, MO, October 2007; Mihir A. Desai, Fritz Foley, and James R. Hines Jr., "Labor and Capital Shares of the Corporate Tax Burden: International Evidence," Prepared for the International Tax Forum and Urban Institute–Brookings Institution Tax Policy Center Conference on Who Pays the Corporate Tax in an Open Economy; Li Liu and Rosanne Altshuler, "Measuring the Burden of the Corporate Income Tax under Imperfect Competition," *National Tax Journal* 66, no. 1 (March 2013): 215–38.

In contrast, other scholars adopt assumptions about the international market being perfectly competitive, where labor bears a larger portion of corporate income tax owing to the ability of corporations to move capital across countries (see table 4.2).

Of course, markets are not perfectly competitive, and capital is not completely mobile. In their frequently cited 1963 book, Marian Krzyaniak and Richard Musgrave find that after-tax profits rise in the short run in response to increases in the corporate income tax.[7] According to University of California–Berkeley economist Alan Auerbach, taxation on capital in an imperfect market further restricts output: "[A] tax on production in an industry in which output is already restricted by imperfect competition will be more distortionary than one in a competitive environment, because it exacerbates an already existing distortion."[8] As a result, the US share of global corporate capital will decline in the long run in response to less burdensome corporate tax rates abroad. A rising burden on corporate capital discourages capital formation in the United States and lowers wages and economic growth. In a 2012 paper, economists Ergete Ferede and Bev Dahlby cite a 2010 publication of the Organisation for Economic Co-operation and Development that claims that corporate income taxes "have the most adverse effect on per capita GDP growth followed by personal income and consumption taxes."[9]

To encourage capital formation in the United States and promote higher wages and economic growth, federal tax policy reform should deal with the increasingly high statutory US corporate tax rate, especially compared to the rates of other countries (see figure 4.1; see also chapter 3). The historical trend suggests that international markets are clearly becoming more competitive, not less (see figures 4.2 and 4.3, pages 90 and 92). Consequentially, the data indicate that the trend

Figure 4.1. Corporate Income Tax Rates in Organisation of Economic Co-operation and Development Countries, 2000 and 2013

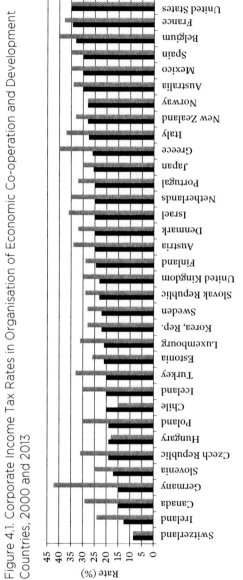

■ Corporate income tax rate - 2013   ▦ Corporate income tax rate - 2000

Source: OECD, "Taxation of Corporate and Capital Income," table II.1, Paris, May 2013.

is toward labor bearing more of the corporate tax burden. As chapter 3 explains, instead of retaining high statutory tax rates on corporations, which will likely increase capital flight, tax policy reform should lower the US corporate tax rate.[10]

However, neither the effective rate of tax on corporate income nor the statutory rate can fully explain the economic distortions caused by the federal tax system. Another cause for economic inefficiencies is the complexity of the US tax code. A 2013 paper by Hans Bacher and Marius Brülhart finds that the complexity of a corporate tax code is a significant determinant in the rate of new businesses being formed.[11] As chapter 1 explains, the complexity of the US tax code costs the economy $215 billion to $987 billion annually. Preferential treatment of debt financing is another determinant of economic inefficiency, often exacerbated by a high corporate income tax rate. A 2010 paper by Simeon Djankov, Tim Ganser, Caralee McLiesh, Rita Ramalho, and Andrei Shleifer finds a significant positive association between the effective corporate tax rate and the ratio of aggregate debt to equity.[12]

Given the significant differences worldwide in corporate income tax rates, owners of capital have many choices regarding which industries to invest in and where to locate geographically. As long as these domestic and international trends continue to reveal an increased sensitivity of corporate capital, a continued decline can be expected in returns on investments in capital-intensive industries in the US corporate sector. We turn now to a detailed discussion of Jennifer

Gravelle's five drivers of capital sensitivity to corporate taxation.

DRIVER 1: HIGH INTERNATIONAL PRODUCT SUBSTITUTION

The elasticity of product substitution assesses the percentage change in demand for an imported good versus a domestically produced good in response to a price change. Jane Gravelle and Kent Smetters's key argument for why corporate capital must bear a high portion of the cost of corporate taxation is that demand substitutability between domestic and foreign tradable goods is low.[13] They claim, in other words, that there are barriers to importing international goods, which in turn protect returns on domestic capital investments in a "closed" economy, thus lowering the corporate income tax burden on labor.

One problem with that argument, as pointed out by William Randolph, is that the data cited to support it examine only the short-run elasticity of international trade substitution.[14] According to Gravelle and Smetters, assuming that capital mobility is high, labor's share of corporate income tax could be as low as 21 percent. If these short-run inelastic numbers indicate US consumers' historical preferences between the same domestically or internationally made product, the levels of US trade as a share of the economy should not increase. However, examination of the continually rising trend of US trade makes clear that these short-run numbers cannot be indicative of actual consumer choices (see figure 4.2).

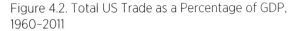

Figure 4.2. Total US Trade as a Percentage of GDP, 1960–2011

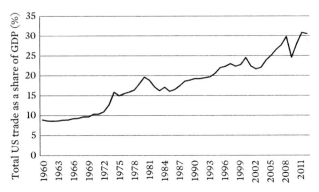

Source: Data from US Census Bureau, Foreign Trade Division, "U.S. Trade in Goods and Services—Balance of Payments (BOP) Basis," June 4, 2013.

Note: Total US trade = US exports + US imports.

Trade's rising share of the US economy reveals that Americans more frequently find that their preferred product was produced abroad rather than at home. Although alternative elasticity numbers are not provided here, this chapter argues that the long-term preference of US consumers is a more convincing measure of US consumer preferences.

Rising levels of trade mean that consumers have more choices than ever. Although a historical argument could be made that relatively low levels of international trade were once small enough that they did not affect corporate decision making regarding where to invest globally for the highest returns on capital, this narrative is unraveling as total trade is growing as a share of US GDP. Products made in foreign markets are becoming increasingly competitive with American products, and the ease with which capital flows across borders is increasing.

DRIVERS 2 AND 3: HIGH GDP AND CAPITAL MOBILITY

The incidence of the corporate income tax that is borne by capital owners depends on how easily capital in the United States can be moved to other countries and on the existing level of capital in a given country relative to the rest of the world. The more easily capital can leave the country for investments with higher payouts, the more heavily American workers will bear the cost of corporate taxation. Part of the problem with the taxation of capital is that at some level it discourages the very formation of capital—startups or a new branch are instead opened in a more tax-competitive country. In separate works, Jane Gravelle and Kent Smetters, Jennifer Gravelle, and William Randolph examine the size of a country's GDP as an explanatory measure for determining the incidence of taxation between labor and capital.[15] James Melvin likewise claims that a country's relative size of GDP may affect international prices.[16] The theory is that the larger a country's market is (as approximated by GDP), the greater the country's ability to determine factor prices by determining the price of the good or service for sale.[17] Randolph finds that the US economy accounted for 30 percent of the world economy,[18] and Jennifer Gravelle uses Randolph's numbers to assert that the United States possesses 30 percent of the world's capital stock.[19] Although the United States used to possess

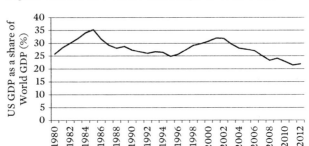

Figure 4.3. US GDP as a Percentage of World GDP

Source: Data from International Monetary Fund, World Economic Outlook Database, April 2013.

more than 50 percent of the world's capital stock,[20] a rapidly growing foreign market has meant that the US share has shrunk relative to that of international competitors (see figure 4.3). International markets are pulling new capital away to more competitive policy environments.

It can be concluded from figures 4.2 and 4.3 that foreign markets have become more competitive. Not only is international trade more prevalent than at any other time in US history (meaning that US consumers are more frequently buying abroad, and that foreign consumers are more frequently buying US goods), but also an increasing number of consumers worldwide also can afford to buy products (meaning that the importance of being within US borders to be close to consumers is decreasing). As markets become more internationally competitive with one another, national corporate tax policy becomes a more important determinant of the level and location of a business's capital investments.

Even under assumptions of imperfect competition, the continued decline in relative US GDP suggests that the ability of the United States to set prices will become more limited as world GDP rises—making the United States more of a price taker than a price setter. As a result, corporate taxation has implications for businesses that are trying to decide where to increase production, where to locate for new production, and when to add to existing investment. Economists John Mutti and Harry Grubert find production intended for exports to be particularly sensitive to tax differences: if proximity to the market is decreasingly important, the role of tax policy becomes more significant.[21] For businesses that want to locate in foreign countries for new production, effective average tax rates are a significant determinant.[22] Djankov and colleagues find that "a 10 percentage point increase in the first-year effective corporate tax rate reduces the aggregate investment to gross domestic product (GDP) ratio by about 2 percentage points (mean is 21 percent), and the official entry rate by 1.4 percentage points (mean is 8 percent)."[23] Studies by Grubert and Mutti and by James Hines and Eric Rice also find a large negative effect of the average tax rate on capital stock.[24]

Another way to examine whether capital is more mobile today is to determine whether US investors have increased their investments in foreign stocks and bonds. Greater amounts of such investments might suggest that payouts in the international community

Figure 4.4. Ownership of Foreign Equities

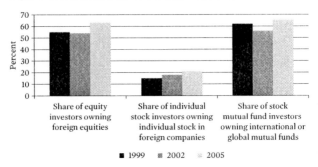

Source: Investment Company Institute and the Securities Industry Association, "Equity Ownership in America," 2005, figure 31.

are rising relative to payouts from US-based firms, all other things being equal. One small set of time series data on statutory combined corporate tax cuts provides additional evidence of greater capital competition (see figure 4.4).

The rising trend in foreign equity ownership might be the result of increased economic growth in foreign countries (increased competition of return), the desire for a more diversified risk portfolio, or the result of the growing noncompetitive nature of a US business relative to a lower-taxed business (as average global tax rates continue to fall). Regardless of the reason, these trends may indicate that the investment choices available to owners of capital are greater now than in the past. To the extent that corporate tax reform can increase the desirability of US equity, tax reform should seek to decrease what has become the highest statutory corporate tax rate among developed countries.

DRIVERS 4 AND 5: HIGH FACTOR SUBSTITUTION AND HIGH DEGREE OF INDUSTRY CAPITAL INTENSITY

Jennifer Gravelle's last two drivers that determine tax incidence are factor substitution and factor intensity. The more competitive markets are, the more these two drivers will be affected by corporate taxation. *Factor substitution* is a measurement of how easily businesses can exchange labor for capital over time, whereas *factor intensity* is a static measurement of how much labor and how much capital a particular industry uses for profits. In separate works, Melvin and Randolph find that the domestic burden of the corporate income tax is borne by the factor used most intensely.[25] For now, labor remains the predominant factor of production for US business profits. Although this chapter does not provide estimates of an elasticity of substitution between capital and labor, in the overall US economy capital is clearly being substituted for labor (see figure 4.5).

One possibility is that the corporate income tax actually drives resources and capital into the noncorporate sector. The model that best examines this idea is a closed economy, where capital can be located only in the corporate or noncorporate sector of a given economy and can neither be created nor destroyed. As economists Mihir Desai, C. Fritz Foley, and James Hines claim:

> If the corporate sector of the economy has a lower capital/labor ratio than the noncorporate

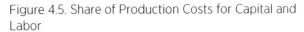

Figure 4.5. Share of Production Costs for Capital and Labor

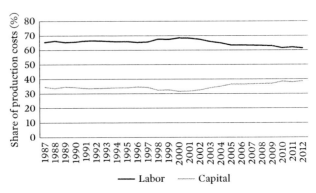

Source: US Bureau of Labor Statistics, "Net Multifactor Productivity and Costs, 1987–2013: Private Business Sector (Excluding Government Enterprises)."

sector, then the introduction of a corporate tax shifts resources into the noncorporate sector and thereby raises the demand for capital. If this effect is large enough, then it has the potential to exceed in magnitude the countervailing impact of factor substitution, thereby implying that higher rates of corporate tax are associated with greater after-tax returns to capital including capital invested in corporations. It would then follow that labor bears the burden of the corporate tax in the form of lower wages.[26]

Hence, one possible interpretation of figure 4.5 is that, in addition to deadweight loss from the economic efficiencies of the corporate tax code, the noncorporate economy is growing in the United States at the expense of growth in the corporate sector. Desai, Foley, and Hines reach a similar conclusion in an open-economy model that follows from using an assumption of perfect capital mobility by which after-tax rates of return on capital cannot differ across countries. Laurence Kotlikoff and Jianjun Miao find that the corporate income tax keeps entrepreneurs from incorporating because of the large fixed costs of public incorporation and that therefore fewer workers are hired.[27] As a result, a number of businesses remain S corporations when they might otherwise become C corporations.

The other possibility, with seemingly more significant economic costs, is that businesses are moving capital to foreign countries. If a business desires to maintain its corporate status, it may move its capital to a foreign market. Whether capital leaves for foreign markets or for the US noncorporate sector, the pressures of corporate taxation increase the ratio of capital to labor in the corporate sector such that capital becomes a relatively more profitable factor of production. Labor, the less marginally productive factor of production, bears the cost of the corporate income tax through falling wages or slower wage growth.

CONCLUSIONS

Jennifer Gravelle presents five drivers for determining whether corporate tax incidence falls on capital or on labor: (a) degree of international product substitution, (b) size of domestic GDP relative to world GDP, (c) degree of international capital mobility,

(d) degree of factor substitution, and (e) degree of capital intensity. Establishing the actual incidence, or who bears the burden of the corporate income tax, is significant because only then will policymakers have the knowledge to understand whether capital in the US corporate sector is able to grow or is pressured to leave (either internationally or domestically to the noncorporate sector). Additionally, policymakers can then better understand who exactly is being taxed when an increase in corporate income taxes is being considered. For example, if the burden of the corporate tax falls primarily on labor, proposals to raise the corporate income tax are really a call to raise taxes on workers, not the owners of capital. This realization would deepen policymakers' understanding of the progressive or regressive nature of various tax reform proposals.

Contrary to Jennifer Gravelle's assertion that demand substitutability between domestic and foreign tradable goods is low, the upward trend in US trade as a percentage of GDP is clear (see figure 4.2, page 90). Trade as a percentage of GDP has risen from less than 10 percent to more than 30 percent as of 2011. US corporations are reaching international markets, and international producers are better able than ever to reach US consumers. US consumers now use more international products than at any other time, thereby decreasing the importance of American-made products.

The level of US capital relative to that of the rest of the world is falling. The United States, which once held more than 50 percent of the world's capital, now holds less than 25 percent (see figure 4.3, page 92). These decreasing numbers mean that the importance of a corporation being located close to the US market is lower than ever.

Empirical studies show that a country's level of capital investment is sensitive to the effective corporate tax rate and that investors are increasing the level of international capital in their portfolios. In other words, new businesses gravitate toward friendlier tax policies, and US investors are increasingly investing overseas.

Factor substitution of capital for labor is increasing, whereas labor intensity, although trending lower, remains high (see figure 4.5, page 96). *Factor substitution* measures how easily a business can exchange labor for capital (or vice versa) over time, whereas *factor intensity* is a static measurement of how much labor or capital a certain industry uses in the course of making profits.

With growing levels of product substitution, relatively lower US GDP as a share of the world's GDP, high international capital mobility, the ability to use less labor in total production costs (factor substitution), and the high use of labor to produce corporate receipts, all five indicators provided by Jennifer Gravelle point to an economy in which labor bears more of the burden of corporate taxation than is traditionally accepted in the current literature.

CHAPTER 5
How Does the Corporate Tax Code Distort Capital Investments?

The current US tax code is complex, carved up by special interests, and full of distortionary tax rates that treat similar activities unequally. Unequal taxation inefficiently distorts consumer and investor decisions, which can be damaging to the economy. These problems are particularly egregious in the tax system that applies to corporate capital investments. This chapter looks at the way the US tax code currently deals with capital investments, some inefficiencies, and possible alternative solutions. The tax code requires that most new purchases of capital, such as machines and buildings, be deducted from total revenue over the course of many years—this is called *depreciation* or *capital cost recovery*. Unequal tax rates develop across industries because of disparities in when the tax is paid. A one-dollar investment today can be reduced to as little as 37 cents of real write-off value, diminishing the profitability of investments.[1]

Using IRS data for 11 different industries from 1998 to 2010, this chapter provides individual effective

This chapter was written by Jason J. Fichtner and Adam N. Michel.

tax rates for each industry (see appendix). Driven primarily by current depreciation policies, capital investments of C corporations are taxed unequally, at effective rates as high as 36.9 percent and as low as 9.2 percent.[2]

As a solution to the current inequity and inefficiency in depreciation policies, this chapter advocates full expensing. Expensing offers an even ground for capital investments by allowing businesses to write off all expenditures in the year they are purchased, resulting in a zero effective rate on equity-financed capital investment. A zero effective rate refers to the expected tax rate paid on an investment that breaks even (does not turn a profit). This proposal does not alter the corporate income tax rate or the tax rates for capital gains and dividends. Expensing simplifies the tax code, reduces the ability to gain targeted tax favors, and increases investment. Some short-run costs that are associated with expensing may need to be paid in order to get to a better overall tax policy, but expensing in the long run is likely to be revenue neutral or to even enhance growth and revenue.[3]

WHY DEPRECIATE ASSETS?

Investments with any capital intensity require purchasing machinery, software, property, or structures. The accounting practice of depreciation was first instituted when businesses were reporting earnings to shareholders: without depreciation, years with large investment purchases would show negative profits, and years with no investments would show high profits, all else being equal. To reduce these swings in reported earnings and convey a business's true position, accountants distribute the cost of each investment over the number of years it will be in service. This practice is called *depreciation* or *cost recovery*. Accountants depreciate a given asset by deducting a set percentage of an investment each year until the carried balance is zero.[4] This method of depreciation, commonly used in book accounting, communicates profitability to shareholders but distorts the profitability of capital investments when applied to the US tax code.[5]

This chapter will refer to depreciation when applied to the tax code as *tax depreciation*. Tax depreciation is important because the timing of cost recovery can mean significant differences in how much tax revenue is collected in a given year and over time, owing to inflation and the time value of money.[6] Investment decisions are made on the basis of after-tax profitability, which is directly affected by how an asset is depreciated. The timing of depreciation and its effect on profitability are explored later in this chapter. Historically, the tax code has allowed several different tax methods for calculating cost-recovery schedules.

Straight-line depreciation divides the total cost of an asset by its useful life (where useful life is either estimated or set arbitrarily) and deducts the same yearly amount over the asset's life. For example, a $1,000 piece of equipment that will be used for five years would be written off 20 percent, or $200 each year for five years. The complicated part of all depreciation methods is determining the useful life of the piece of equipment or structure.[7] In the US tax code, these depreciation time lines are defined by asset classes, in which similar goods are grouped together.[8]

Declining-balance depreciation, known more generally as *accelerated depreciation*, uses similar asset classes as those used by straight-line depreciation but allows more of the original cost to be deducted up front. In a stylized version of accelerated depreciation, 40 percent of a $1,000 piece of equipment would be deducted in the first year, 40 percent of the remaining balance in the second year, and so on. In the fifth year, the remaining cost would be written off.[9] Depreciation can also be accelerated by arbitrarily shortening the depreciation time line. The term *accelerated depreciation* does not offer great specificity; it refers generally to faster cost recovery than allowed by straight-line depreciation with accurate time lines.[10]

DEPRECIATION ALLOWANCES: A BRIEF HISTORY

The debate over how best to define the useful life of an asset began in the mid-1900s. From the time of the corporate income tax's implementation in 1909 through 1942, businesses were allowed to depreciate assets as they saw fit.[11] In 1954, the US government officially recognized the use of accelerated depreciation and continued its use until 1962, when a new and more rigid set of guidelines was enacted.[12] Depreciation time lines and asset classes were further crystalized through industry-wide surveys in 1971.[13] The

Economic Recovery Tax Act of 1981 first strayed from previous depreciation schemes by shortening asset lives with little consideration of the facts and circumstances of estimated useful lives.[14]

The most recent major modification to the US depreciation guidelines was included in the Tax Reform Act of 1986, which set up two different systems of depreciation: the modified accelerated cost-recovery system (MACRS) and the alternative depreciation system (ADS).[15] A majority of assets are depreciated using MACRS, which generally stipulates shorter asset lives and uses accelerated depreciation.[16] ADS is used for assets that are not eligible for MACRS. It uses straight-line depreciation with asset lives that are generally longer than those under MACRS.[17]

Accelerated depreciation for tax purposes was originally justified because it more closely mimics declining productivity as equipment ages.[18] Depending on use, maintenance, and environment, two similar pieces of machinery can depreciate at very different rates. Compounded by inflation, developing a proper depreciation schedule for every investment is a difficult task. In modern policy debates, accelerated depreciation has most often been put forth as an investment incentive. Policy advocates often use this justification to argue for bonus depreciation.

First used in 2002, additional first-year depreciation deductions have been enacted to stimulate both investment and the economy.[19] Bonus depreciation allows a one-time deduction of 30 to 100 percent of the initial cost of an investment in the year of purchase. These special tax incentives are available for a limited time and often target specific types of investment. Provisions were enacted in 2002, 2003, 2004, 2008, 2009, 2010, and 2012.[20]

Accelerated depreciation, including bonus depreciation, has received attention because it is the largest corporate tax expenditure.[21] The Government Accountability Office estimates that accelerated depreciation of machinery and equipment reduced taxes by $76.1 billion in 2011, an estimated 42 percent of total corporate income tax revenue.[22] The perceived size of the expenditure has made depreciation a much-discussed candidate for tax reform, with various advocates arguing for manipulating it in order to lower the statutory corporate tax rate, increase federal revenue, or further stimulate investment.[23]

DEPRECIATION TODAY

Two types of reforms to the depreciation system have been proposed in the tax literature: (a) change the timing of depreciation schedules, and (b) allow full expensing. Changing depreciation timing by lengthening schedules, moving to a straight-line method, or using some other means of slowing accelerated depreciation would, all else being equal, increase tax revenue. Expensing allows all companies to write off the full cost of their investments in the year purchased, thereby lowering the effective corporate tax rate and benefiting investment. It is worth noting that some proposals to change the timing of depreciation attempt to remain revenue neutral by simultaneously calling for lower statutory corporate tax rates. The projected revenue increases from depreciating assets over a longer period of time are used to offset projected revenue losses from lower statutory corporate tax rates.

On its face, eliminating accelerated depreciation for a straight-line method seems simple. Complications arise when determining on what schedule assets should be depreciated. One example from economist Jane Gravelle analyzes a switch of all assets from the MACRS to the longer, straight-line depreciation schedules of the ADS.[24] In exchange for the revenue increases from slower depreciation, Gravelle finds that revenue-neutral tax reform could be achieved by cutting the statutory corporate tax rate by, at most, 4.7 percentage points—which would mean a new corporate tax rate of 30.3 percent. However, the amount of the cut shrinks to 1.6 percentage points when the forecasting horizon is expanded beyond the typical 10 years.[25] The time horizon matters because depreciation policy only shifts the timing of taxes paid. When depreciation schedules are lengthened (moving tax payments forward in time), inflation and time discounts on money result in larger tax collections.

A more modest proposal to slow depreciation was put forward by the Congressional Budget Office (CBO).[26] CBO explains that most depreciation rates were calculated in 1986, assuming 5 percent inflation. However, for the next decade, CBO predicts 2.3 percent inflation, which skews the current depreciation time lines, making the deduction more valuable and lowering real federal revenue. The proposal extends each asset class's life but leaves the methods of declining-balance depreciation the same.[27]

By extending the period for depreciation, CBO's proposal attempts to bring the effective tax rates for equipment and structures into parity by more accurately matching tax time lines and useful lives.[28]

The second major tax reform proposal is immediate cost recovery, or full expensing. Expensing allows a business to deduct the full cost of a new investment from its taxable income in the year it was purchased. One might think of full expensing as enacting a permanent 100 percent bonus depreciation. Expensing capital costs is similar to the current tax treatment of an investment in labor. Just as training costs are deductible from taxable corporate income, full expensing would deduct outlays for equipment from taxable income. Expensing lowers taxes on new capital investments to zero, simplifies the tax code, and treats all types of investment similarly.

EXPANDING THE CASE FOR EXPENSING

Although expensing does not lower the statutory corporate tax rate, it does lower the effective rate. Expensing eliminates corporate taxes specific to capital investments, but it does not change taxes on capital gains, dividends, interest, or general corporate income. Economist Stephen Entin illustrates the implicit tax on investments under the current system of depreciation by showing how the present value of the tax write-off is reduced. If a one-dollar investment is expensed immediately, the business receives one full dollar as a tax write-off. In the case of a one-dollar investment being depreciated over 39 years (as some structures are), assuming 3 percent inflation that dollar would receive a write-off worth only 37 cents in present value. This example shows that the tax requirement to depreciate investments over time also diminishes the value of the write-off. The decrease in value is felt disproportionately on investments that have long useful lives and is compounded by uncertainty stemming from unknown long-run expectations about inflation.[29]

If a business were forced to move from expensing to depreciation, there would be a similar effect to the previously described decrease in the present-value write-off. Relative to expensing, depreciation requires accelerated tax payments. A business has not made a profit until revenue exceeds costs. When businesses are required to pay taxes before they turn a profit, the government essentially secures an interest-free loan by receiving tax payments on profit not yet earned. By eliminating complex depreciation systems, expensing decreases the effective rate of taxation on capital investment to zero because there is no time over which the deduction can lose value.[30]

Expensing is an investment incentive for new capital investment. Unlike an across-the-board tax rate reduction, expensing lowers the taxes paid on future investments rather than on all profits earned from new and old capital. A zero effective rate on capital investments increases the after-tax rate of return on new investments, making them more attractive under expensing.[31]

To fully realize the goal of a flat zero rate on all capital investments, one must acknowledge the disproportionate tax rates of debt- and equity-financed investment. Although this chapter does not tackle the issue of interest deductions, the issue merits a brief discussion given the broader theme of a less distortionary tax code. Effective tax rates for debt- and equity-financed capital are −6.4 and 36.1 percent, respectively, as calculated in a 2005 CBO paper.[32] CBO estimates that full expensing would result in an effective rate of −87.5 percent for debt-financed investments and a zero percent rate for equity-financed capital investments.[33] This case illustrates the strong incentives for debt-financed investments that currently exist under the US tax code.

Depending on how the tax base is defined, a properly neutral tax treatment of interest should allow all interest to be deducted if such interest is taxable or no interest to be deducted if the interest is not considered taxable.[34] Any future comprehensive tax reform must address the role that taxation of interest and interest deductions should play in the tax code.

It should also be recognized that under current depreciation policies, even within a single industry, there is a gap in effective tax rates between tangible and intangible investments and between different types of equipment and structures.[35] The US tax code treats intangible assets in many different and seemingly unequal ways. Intangible assets consist of a variety of nonphysical goods: patents, copyrights, brand names, databases, and labor. In many cases, some intangible assets are immediately expensed.[36] For example, imagine a business pays an employee to compile a valuable data bank of searchable information. The employee's wages are expensed, as are most other operating costs. However, the purchase of a new server for the data bank must be depreciated over several years. The current US tax code favors certain types of investment over others. Expensing treats all investments similarly.

There are large discrepancies in effective tax rates within tangible asset classes. In 2005, CBO estimated the average effective corporate tax rate on investments as 26.3 percent, ranging from 36.9 percent on computers and peripheries to 9.2 percent on petroleum and natural gas structures.[37] The variations in tax rates generally result from depreciation rules that differ from the actual useful life:

> The top quartile [of effective rates] consists entirely of computers and peripheral equipment, inventories, manufacturing buildings, and land. The bottom quartile contains 19 different asset types. The major asset types with the lowest rates are mining structures, petroleum and natural-gas structures, railroad equipment, aircraft, specialized industrial machinery, fabricated metal products, ships and boats, and construction machinery.[38]

A shift to full expensing would decrease differences in effective tax rates across industries by treating equipment and buildings—tangible assets—in a manner more similar to the way intangible assets are treated.

A reform to full expensing would increase the quantity of investments by increasing the after-tax profit of investments. Investments, which carry inherent risk, must be expected to earn back their costs, plus the rate of inflation and a premium for the risk of the investment, or the investor will choose a different option.[39] Depreciation for tax purposes overstates simple pretax profit calculations because the present value of the write-off is less than the full cost of the investment.[40] The overstated profits increase taxable income, thereby resulting in higher effective tax rates and lower rates of return on investments. However, expensing does not shelter any profit from taxation—all revenue, after an investment is paid off, is taxed at the statutory rate. Expensing allows the full cost of investments to be recovered, thus inducing more investment and expanding the economy.[41]

RENT-SEEKING

Beyond the direct economic effects of expensing, it would simplify the tax code. As discussed previously, the effective tax rate on standard corporate investments ranges from 9.2 to 36.9 percent—a 27.7 percentage point spread in the taxation of different asset types, primarily driven by uneven depreciation policy. Requiring assets to be depreciated instead of expensed results in winners and losers, thereby allowing the tax code to hurt some industries and help others. The ability to manipulate depreciation for special tax breaks also opens the door to rent-seeking. Congress has the ability to alter the standard MACRS depreciation periods through statutory changes that apply to specific types of assets. A 2012 report by the

Joint Committee on Taxation lists 55 separate statutory changes to MACRS depreciation periods.[42] The list details changes to the class lives of racehorses, a natural gas pipeline in Alaska, green energy property and equipment, magazine circulation expenditures, research and development, and intangible drilling costs.[43] Many of these special provisions give a specific industry or production method a tax-favored status for its investments.

Rent-seeking opportunities encourage corporations to spend money to lobby Congress for special tax breaks.[44] Money spent on lobbying does not create anything new or move the economy forward—such rent-seeking holds the economy back.[45] Any form of tax depreciation will always be subject to political manipulation. Switching to full expensing eliminates the ability to alter tax depreciation time lines to the advantage of politically favored industries.

Because expensing would simplify the US tax code, it would also lessen administrative costs. A Laffer Center study on the economic burden of tax code complexities found that US businesses spend 2.94 billion hours complying with the federal tax code, at a cost of $216.2 billion annually. Taxpayers in aggregate spend the equivalent of 30 percent of total income taxes collected trying to comply with the tax code.[46] According to the Laffer Center, the low-end estimate of a 50 percent reduction in tax code complexity would increase the country's annual economic growth rate by 0.45 percentage points over 10 years.[47] Expensing could help reduce complexity and facilitate some portion of the noted efficiency gains. As Nobel laureate and economics professor Vernon Smith notes, "Perhaps the most valuable advantage of fully expensing capital outlays is that of introducing administrative and clerical simplicity where there has tended to exist great complication."[48]

Alan Auerbach and Dale Jorgenson comment on the efficiency gains from removing the administrative burden of depreciation by noting that businesses could eliminate entire sections of their tax accounting staff if they were no longer required to factor tax depreciation into yearly tax liability reporting and long-run investment decisions.[49] Chief financial officers also prefer a less complicated tax code. A 2011 Duke University–CFO Magazine survey found that 70 percent of chief financial officers would give up all tax exemptions for tax code simplicity, even though their companies might not come out ahead.[50]

REVENUE EFFECTS OF EXPENSING

Federal tax policy that allows expensing is more efficient and equitable across different industries. Revenue projections are less certain. Entin lays out a simplified illustration of switching from straight-line depreciation for a $100 piece of equipment over five years to expensing, assuming that a business purchases one new $100 piece of equipment each year. Old assets will be allowed to depreciate under the old law, and new purchases will be expensed. In year 1, the business gets an additional $80 write-off; in year 2, $60; in year 3, $40; in year 4, $20; and in year 5, the business would be back to its initial $100 yearly write-off.

In the short run, expensing would decrease federal revenue. Over time, revenue would stabilize back to its old levels.[51] Auerbach corroborates Entin's assessment, writing that, "to allow expensing net of corporate borrowing . . . is likely to have a small net impact on revenue, at least in the long run."[52]

Entin and Auerbach's discussions of revenue do not completely account for the growth effects of full expensing. There would be economic growth from efficiency gains owing to simplicity, better returns on investments, and reduced rent-seeking as a result of signaling that the US tax code is less open to exemption tampering. Expensing would make each new asset "more attractive and have a higher rate of return. The capital stock as well as private sector incomes and wages will rise, and revenues will improve."[53] Furthermore, the federal government has already absorbed much of the transition cost as a result of past bonus depreciation tax incentives.[54] If an expensing policy were to be enacted today, small revenue losses would likely occur in the short run, and modest revenue increases in the long run.[55]

On a static basis, where growth effects are not taken into account, tax expensing will not be revenue neutral. However, because expensing makes investment relatively more attractive, it can reasonably be assumed that some growth effects will result from the tax change. An estimate of the growth effects from full expensing by the Tax Foundation finds that "full expensing would increase GDP by 5.13 percent, lift the capital stock by 15.4 percent, raise wages by 4.36 percent, create 885,300 jobs, and boost federal revenue by

$121.3 billion" in the long run.[56] Although the tax revenue picture is not easily projected, the static projections of lost revenue are almost certainly incorrect. By lowering the effective tax rate on capital investments, expensing will remove the current tax disadvantage on investments. In relative terms, under a system with full expensing, investors would find investments (future consumption) more attractive than current consumption. Increased investment has the potential to raise the economic growth rate in both the long run and the short run. In other words, the long-run revenue effects depend on how much extra investment is actually induced by moving to a system of full tax expensing and how much tax revenue is then gained at the margin from increased GDP.

DIFFERENCES IN INDUSTRY'S SENSITIVITY TO CHANGES IN DEPRECIATION ALLOWANCES

By using the IRS's Statistics of Income data for active corporations for 1998–2010, we are able to estimate which industries would be most sensitive to changes in depreciation (see table 5.1).[57] The calculations presented in table 5.1 show how the removal of existing depreciation policies would affect the tax rates of 11 industries. The calculation is made by removing the current depreciation deduction from total deductions, adding it to total income subject to tax, and applying the effective tax rate. Historical effective tax rates, by industry, are provided in the appendix.

Although the method of analysis used here is imprecise because of data limitations, removing

Table 5.1. Effect of Depreciation on Effective Tax Rates

INDUSTRY	EFFECTIVE RATE WITHOUT DEPRECIATION (%)	HISTORIC EFFECTIVE RATE (%)	DIFFERENCE (PERCENTAGE POINTS)
Mining	28.47	21.28	7.19
Manufacturing	25.29	19.48	5.81
Information	32.18	27.96	4.22
Utilities	33.73	30.34	3.39
Transportation and warehousing	33.50	31.09	2.41
Wholesale trade	31.81	30.16	1.65
Agriculture, forestry, fishing, and hunting	28.40	27.31	1.09
Finance and insurance	31.28	30.33	0.96
Retail trade	32.78	32.06	0.72
Construction	31.52	30.95	0.56
Health care and social assistance	33.44	32.94	0.50

Source: Data from Internal Revenue Service, "Table 12—Returns of Active Corporations, Other than Forms 1120-REIT, 1120-RIC, and 1120S" (1998–2012). June 27, 2014. Detail may not add owing to rounding.

depreciation from deductions helps illustrate how each industry's tax status is distorted by the current US tax code. A move to expensing would lower the effective rate; table 5.1 shows the percentage point change between the current or historic effective rate and the new, higher effective tax rate without depreciation and existing bonus depreciation for 11 industries. The higher effective rates reflect a tax situation that is more similar to paying taxes on all income without deducting investment costs. A larger change represents a more sensitive industry.[58]

The calculation illustrates each industry's sensitivity to the elimination of depreciation and bonus depreciation. Table 5.1 also shows how depreciation and bonus depreciation lower the effective rate disproportionately across different industries. Because depreciation might be viewed as the consumption of depreciable investments, industries toward the top of the table would likely stand to gain much from expensing policies that would reduce the effective tax rate without depreciation. Figure 5.1 illustrates the difference between the current effective tax rate and the new effective rate without depreciation.

The pressures that the highly sensitive industries face under current cost-recovery rules are mirrored by CBO's list of assets occupying the bottom quartile of effective rates: mining structures, petroleum and natural gas structures, railroad equipment, aircraft, specialized industrial machinery, fabricated metal products, ships and boats, and construction machinery.[59] These assets are heavily used in table 5.1's five most sensitive industries. The low rates on these assets

Figure 5.1. Effect of Depreciation on Effective Tax Rates

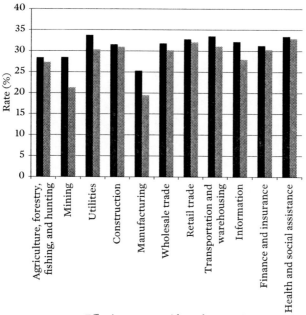

■ Effective tax rate without depreciation
▓ Historic effective tax rate

Source: Data from Internal Revenue Service, "Table 12—Returns of Active Corporations, Other than Forms 1120-REIT, 1120-RIC, and 1120S" (1998–2012), June 27, 2014.

may signal that associated industries are highly motivated to lobby for faster accelerated depreciation.

Table 5.2 shows how capital intensive each industry is in terms of depreciation as a percentage of corporate income subject to tax. For some industries, the annual use of depreciation exceeds total income on a yearly basis. Interestingly, the industries that are highly capital intensive (table 5.2) are not necessarily

Table 5.2. Industry Reliance on Depreciable Capital

INDUSTRY	CAPITAL INTENSITY RATIO (%)
Utilities	237
Transportation and warehousing	220
Agriculture, forestry, fishing, and hunting	168
Information	138
Mining	104
Health care and social assistance	101
Wholesale trade	71
Construction	67
Manufacturing	62
Retail trade	57
Finance and insurance	23

Source: Data from Internal Revenue Service, "Table 12—Returns of Active Corporations, Other than Forms 1120-REIT, 1120-RIC, and 1120S" (1998–2012), June 27, 2014.

the industries that are most sensitive to shifts in cost recovery (table 5.1). The sensitivity ranking is most likely picking up the size of the depreciation deduction relative to all other frequently used deductions and credits across a given industry.

This chapter suggests that industries that are more sensitive to changes in capital cost recovery will likely benefit the most from full expensing. The intersection of CBO's lowest asset rates and the industries ranked here as highly sensitive indicates which industries have the greatest incentive to lobby for special tax treatment. The industries at the bottom of table 5.1 should not be dismissed, though, as potential beneficiaries of immediate cost recovery because all industries will benefit from full expensing in absolute terms.

CRITIQUES OF FULL COST RECOVERY

The US corporate tax system is riddled with inefficiencies. Full expensing is just one of many changes that would make the US tax code more efficient and equitable. Any proposed change to the tax code will have detractors with well-formed critiques. This section addresses common objections to expensing. Full expensing on its own is not a magic tax code remedy; it should be part of a larger reform.

The first objection to expensing is that businesses should be arguing for statutory rate reduction instead. Tom Neubig, national director of quantitative economics and statistics at Ernst & Young, gives seven reasons corporate finance and tax officers prefer lower corporate tax rates to expensing.[60] His critique assumes a binary choice: either expensing or lower tax rates, but not both. Additionally, as J. D. Foster argues, "Even capital-intensive firms often appear to prefer lower tax rates to more accelerated depreciation."[61] It is important to note that the case presented in this chapter for expensing is not an argument against lower statutory tax rates, although Gravelle's paper on long-run revenue collections may temper enthusiasm for statutory rate reform.[62] However, in contrast with rate reduction and a focus on the tax treatment of capital, expensing brings rates of taxation on all capital goods into parity and increases the return on capital investments.[63] The fact that the effective rate reduction does not appear in book accounting presents a perception problem that may be hard to overcome, but the economic savings are very real. Furthermore, the 2011 Duke–CFO Magazine survey shows that executives can look beyond some accounting losses if they think they will come out ahead on other margins.[64] The most salient concern for some businesses is a possible change to the interest deduction, although this concern does not constitute a critique of full expensing as a policy in its own right.

A second objection to expensing is that the existing bonus depreciation policy has already failed the litmus test for encouraging investment. Is bonus depreciation an effective tax incentive? The question is important to the discussion here because bonus depreciation is not only a form of accelerated depreciation but also a stepping-stone to full expensing. Federal Reserve Board economist Jesse Edgerton looks at whether accelerated depreciation or an investment tax credit is more effective as an investment incentive.[65] He concludes that accelerated depreciation is about half as effective as an investment tax credit. This effect is weak because accelerated depreciation provisions do not show up in the effective tax rate for book purposes. That rate is a key indicator for investors; thus, corporate executives may be less focused on other measures of effective tax rates.[66] Accounting professors David Hulse and Jane Livingstone compare investment in 2001 and 2004, when bonus depreciation was allowed, to years without bonus depreciation and also find it to be a weak investment incentive.[67] The literature seems to be in general agreement: temporary accelerated and bonus depreciation provisions are middling stimulus measures.[68]

Despite the consensus that bonus depreciation is not a strong investment incentive, expensing has some important differences that may produce different results. Temporary bonus depreciation is intended to shift investment forward rather than induce a higher level of total investment.[69] Furthermore, the temporary provisions are often only 30 to 50 percent. The small effects found in papers examining bonus depreciation might increase significantly if the provision were expanded to 100 percent and made permanent. Expensing removes much of the uncertainty from the current depreciation system, which offers a parade of temporary write-offs and exemptions. Businesses generally make large-scale investment decisions on the basis of long-run economic considerations, not the temporary vicissitudes of congressional tax tampering.[70]

A more stable tax regime will allow businesses to focus on more productive pursuits and plan for the future with tax certainty.[71] As one of the authors of this chapter has pointed out in testimony before Congress, "Predictable tax policy is essential to long-term economic growth. Generally, temporary tax provisions should be avoided, especially when trying to correct or rectify a permanent problem. Further, allowing any provisions that favor one group or activity over another not only puts the government in the position of picking winners and losers, but also opens the Congress up to be influenced by those seeking special favors."[72]

A third objection to moving to a full expensing system is uncertainty about the policy's revenue neutrality. Although much evidence supports the narrative that, in the long run, expensing will not be a net drain on federal revenue, any tax proposal can have unanticipated revenue effects.[73] This possibility may be an acceptable risk in return for a better tax code. A reduction in rent-seeking opportunities will allow businesses to allocate those dollars to value-creating enterprises, and parity in effective capital tax rates will allow investments to more efficiently flow to their highest-valued use.

CONCLUSION

The complexity and breadth of the US tax code can make any change seem trivial on its own. Expensing may be one of many necessary tools to move toward better federal corporate tax policy. Expensing may have some short-run costs, but they are outweighed by the long-run gains in efficiency, fairness, and economic growth. Effective tax rates influence how businesses allocate their investments, and a flat zero rate on all investments will allow more efficient economic allocation.

Moving away from depreciation toward full expensing will not be an easy sell to stakeholders. Many industries enjoy their favored tax status, and many politicians enjoy the ability to hand out favorable depreciation schedules. Expensing should be an easy sell to those who have an eye on future economic growth. Full cost recovery will help move away from distortionary taxes that have biased investors against long-lived investments, such as manufacturing plants and commercial buildings. Lower effective tax rates would be a boon for investment and would help stimulate domestic economic growth.[74] These changes might shake up some privileged industries, but almost everyone will be better off with an efficient and equitable tax treatment of capital investments.

Finally, as discussed at length in chapters 3 and 4, policymakers must take in account that any corporate tax is a tax on individuals—whether investors, workers, or consumers. Although abolishing the corporate tax code may not be politically feasible at this time, adopting expensing over depreciation is a step in the right direction.

CHAPTER 6

Why Should Congress Reform the Mortgage Interest Deduction?

onsumer advocates view the mortgage interest deduction (MID) as a benefit for lower- and
middle-income taxpayers.[1] Yet fewer than
9.8 percent of tax filers earning less than $50,000
claim the MID, and these are the same households
that would gain the most from the social benefits of
homeownership. Instead, most of the monetary benefits from the MID go to high-income earners, whose
average tax benefit from the MID is nearly nine times
greater than that of households earning $50,000 to
$100,000.

This chapter examines two fundamental problems
with the MID. First, as currently structured, the MID
does not encourage greater homeownership, although
it does encourage higher levels of debt and borrowing.
The primary beneficiaries of tax-subsidized interest
payments on housing are high-income earners, who
are more likely to own homes in the first place. Second,
the MID creates economic inefficiencies, particularly
among high-income taxpayers, who divert resources
from more socially valuable investments into larger
homes. All else being equal, lower levels of economic
efficiency mean fewer jobs and less prosperity.

One of the difficulties with the existing US tax code is that closing one loophole can result in a transfer of much of the government-subsidized spending to a different special tax provision. For example, when the tax deduction for consumer interest was eliminated with the Tax Reform Act of 1986, high-income earners increased their use of housing interest by 67 to 86 cents for every dollar lost in consumer interest.[2] Today, there is still reason to believe that the existing tax bias toward housing is diverting resources from other areas of the economy. Writing about a slightly different tax code in 2005, the US Treasury found that investments in owner-occupied housing had a marginal effective tax rate of nearly 0 percent as a result of capital gains exclusion on the sale of primary residences, whereas investments in noncorporate businesses and corporate businesses were taxed at 17 and 26 percent, respectively.[3] Alan Viard and Robert Carroll find that the existing tax code bias toward housing through the MID diverts resources from other productive investments.[4]

The MID likely could be eliminated with minimal effects on low- and middle-income taxpayers because over 64 percent of the MID tax benefits go to tax filers earning more than $100,000 annually. Eliminating the MID in exchange for lower marginal rates and a higher standard deduction would represent a general improvement in the standard of living for almost all low- and middle-income taxpayers.

However, given the political constraints surrounding repeal of the MID, we also present a second-best option. The MID could be reformed into a nonrefundable credit of approximately $1,070, which would encourage homeownership and provide a stronger tax benefit for low-income households—the households that stand to gain the most from the sociological benefits of homeownership. Adoption of a mortgage interest credit could increase homeownership among low- and middle-income households by as much as 5 percent while decreasing homeownership rates among high-income households by only 1 percent.

WHO BENEFITS FROM THE MORTGAGE INTEREST DEDUCTION?

One of the most commonly cited justifications for the MID is that it promotes homeownership among the middle class and supports industries that employ middle-class workers.[5] About six in every ten Americans oppose elimination of the MID, and one in every four claim it on their income tax returns.[6] By an economic valuation, the MID is a sizable tax subsidy—the third-largest deduction in the US tax code (behind the exclusion of employer contributions for medical insurance premiums and the exclusion of net imputed income). In 2013, the MID decreased federal revenue by $69 billion.[7] Although the upper-middle class does benefit from the deduction, most of the monetary benefits go to higher-income taxpayers and little to none go to low-income households that purchase a home (see figure 6.1). On average, wealthier households borrow more money and have higher rates of homeownership (see figure 6.2, page 132). One reason low-income and many middle-income taxpayers are

Figure 6.1. Benefits of the Mortgage Interest Deduction by Adjusted Gross Income

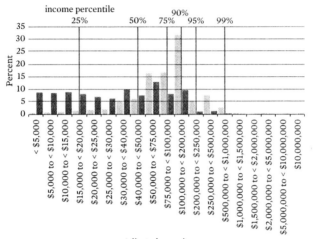

Percentage of reduction in taxable income from MID
Percentage of all tax returns within income bracket

Source: Data from Internal Revenue Service, "Table 1.1—All Returns: Selected Income and Tax Items, by Size and Accumulated Size of Adjusted Gross Income, Tax Year 2010," July 2012, and "Table 3.1—Returns with Modified Taxable Income: Adjusted Gross Income and Tax Items," 2010.

unlikely to use the MID is that the standard deduction for an individual taxpayer in 2014 was $6,200 ($12,400 for married couples filing a joint tax return). Unless annual mortgage interest expenses (combined with any other expenses that are allowed as itemized tax deductions) are greater than the standard deduction, a taxpayer will not opt to itemize deductions. Instead, the taxpayer will take the simpler and more financially sound route of using the standard deduction.[8]

The purported public policy role of housing-related tax deductions and credits is to increase homeownership. In this chapter, we show how much of the MID goes to higher-income earners, who would likely purchase homes even without the MID. Economists Edward Glaeser and Jesse Shapiro reach a similar conclusion—that the MID has little impact on the homeownership rate.[9] As currently structured, the MID fails to significantly increase homeownership among its intended beneficiaries, and it encourages greater debt among homeowners.[10] In short, the MID generally gives a tax break to households that would likely purchase homes anyway and enables high-income households to buy homes that are roughly 10 to 20 percent more expensive than those they would buy otherwise.[11] This chapter does not examine the social benefits of owning a larger home, but a mix of social benefits and costs for homeownership is discussed.

Figure 6.2 shows that the homeownership rate is distinctly higher for households with incomes greater than the median, suggesting that, not surprisingly, income is a significant determinant of ownership. The figure also suggests that the MID is not a significant equalizer of outcome when it comes to homeownership. According to a 1997 paper, 45 percent of the aggregate benefit of the MID went to the 9.8 percent of taxpayers with annual incomes over $100,000.[12] Compared to 1997 nominal household income in 2010, 48.5 percent of the aggregate benefit of the MID goes to 13 percent of taxpayers with incomes over $100,000 (see table 6.2, page 136).[13]

Figure 6.2. Homeownership Rate by Income

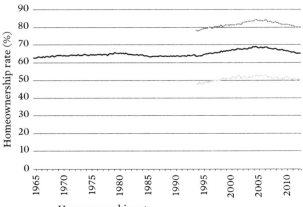

— Homeownership rate

.... Homeownership rate by families with income greater than or equal to median income

..... Homeownership rate by families with income less than median income

Source: Data from the US Census Bureau.

Note: Homeownership rates above and below median family income are not available before 1993.

Many other countries have a mortgage interest deduction, too. Although various social and economic factors contribute to a country's homeownership rate, a side-by-side comparison of countries indicates an inconclusive relationship between the MID and homeownership (see table 6.1). In the United Kingdom, which phased out the MID between 1975 and 2000, the homeownership rate rose from 53 percent in 1974 to 68 percent in 2001.[14] Despite the lack of a statistically strong relationship between tax subsidies and homeownership rates, the United States boasts the world's most generous tax subsidies for

Table 6.1. Homeownership Rates and Mortgage Interest Deductibility for Selected Economies

COUNTRY	HOMEOWNERSHIP RATE (%)	IS MORTGAGE INTEREST DEDUCTIBLE?
Singapore	87	No
Taiwan	84	Yes[a]
Spain	82	Yes
Ireland	77	Yes
Norway	77	Yes
Portugal	75	Yes
Greece	72	Yes[b]
Italy	71	No
Australia	70	No
Canada	68	No
United Kingdom	68	No
New Zealand	67	No
United States	65	Yes
Finland	64	Yes
Belgium	63	Yes[b]
Japan	61	No
Sweden	60	Yes
Poland	59	No[b]
France	55	No[c]
Korea, Rep.	54	No
Netherlands	50	Yes[b]
Austria	49	Yes
Germany	42	No
Switzerland	35	Yes[b]

(continued)

Table 6.1. (*continued*)

Source: Steven C. Bourassa, Donald R. Haurin, Patric H. Hendershott, and Martin Hoesli, "Mortgage Interest Deductions and Homeownership: An International Survey," Research Paper 12-06, Swiss Finance Institute, Geneva, February 9, 2012.
a. Although Taiwan has a mortgage interest deduction, it is tied to another deduction that is available to renters. Steven C. Bourassa and Chieng-Wen Peng, "Why Is Taiwan's Homeownership Rate So High?," *Urban Studies* 48, no. 13 (2011), 2887–904.
b. Greece, Belgium, Poland, the Netherlands, and Switzerland all have imputed rent taxes, although Greece's tax applies only to large dwellings. Calista Cheung, "Policies to Rebalance Housing Markets in New Zealand," OECD Economics Department Working Paper 878, Organisation for Economic Co-operation and Development, 2011.
c. France instated mortgage interest credits for first-time buyers in 2007 but abolished them in 2011.

owner-occupied housing.[15] Much of the justification for the subsidies is focused on encouraging individuals to have better household saving plans. Yet as Yale economist Robert Shiller points out, foreign countries such as Switzerland have higher rates of household savings without high homeownership rates.[16]

A successful tax-favored housing policy would be designed to encourage inframarginal households to purchase a home—people who would like to own homes but who would not do so without a federal subsidy.[17] In 1973, Stanley Surrey, who served as assistant secretary of the treasury for tax policy from 1961 to 1969, wanted to reform the MID to subsidize such households.[18] However, the decision to purchase a home is influenced by a variety of factors, including socioeconomic status and local housing prices. Economists Peter Brady, Julie-Anne Cronin, and Scott

Houser examine some primary factors in the decision to itemize deductions: income, various demographics, and housing prices, as well as federal, state, and local tax policies.[19] They conclude that over 60 percent of the probability of itemizing deductions versus taking the standard deduction is accounted for by regional variation in housing prices and housing tax policies. For many low- and middle-income taxpayers, tax-favored housing policies are often out of reach because the itemized benefit of the MID is not greater than the standard deduction (currently $6,200 for individuals and $12,400 for joint filers). In many cases, using the MID—and any other applicable itemized tax deductions—only makes sense if the taxpayer earns a certain level of income. According to IRS data, three-fourths of tax filers who use the MID have an income of at least $100,000 (see table 6.2). A reform that increased low-income taxpayers' access to tax-favored housing policies would need to take demographics and housing prices into account.

Lowering the marginal tax rates reduces high-income taxpayers' incentive to use the MID. Referring to the 1986 Tax Reform Act, economists James Follain and David Ling say, "All else equal, these reductions in marginal tax rates lower the subsidy to housing."[20] In other words, because such taxpayers are taxed at a lower marginal rate, the MID has less value. As their income increases, taxpayers increasingly benefit from the MID. According to the most recent data, from 2010, households in the bottom 65 percent of the income distribution obtained 18 percent of the reduction in taxable income from the MID, whereas households

Table 6.2. Benefits of the Mortgage Interest Deduction by Income, 2010

	LEVEL OF INCOME		
	UNDER $15,000	$15,000 TO $29,999	$30,000 TO $49,999
Total number of tax returns	35,036,910	30,890,795	25,621,630
Number of itemized tax returns	1,872,849	3,875,849	7,500,859
Number of tax returns claiming MID	1,036,535	2,409,435	5,511,974
Share of tax returns claiming MID (%)	2.96	7.80	21.51
Share of itemized returns claiming MID (%)	55.35	62.17	73.48
Reduction in taxable income from MID ($ thousands)	8,229,943	18,121,315	42,626,632
Reduction in taxable income from MID per return ($)	230	590	1,660
Reduction in taxable income from MID per itemized return ($)	4,390	4,680	5,680
Average reduction in taxable income from MID per returns claiming MID ($)	7,940	7,520	7,730
Effective tax rate for all returns (%)	5.81	6.25	8.83
Effective tax reduction of MID/static revenue loss ($ thousands)	478,263	1,132,671	3,765,705
Effective tax reduction from MID per return	14	37	147

Source: Data from Adrian Dungan and Michael Parisi, "Individual Income Tax Returns, Preliminary Data, 2010," SOI Bulletin 31, no. 3 (Winter 2012): 5–18, 6–8, figure A.

$50,000 TO $99,999	$100,000 TO $199,999	$200,000 TO $249,999	$250,000 AND ABOVE	ALL LEVELS OF INCOME
30,627,721	14,008,889	1,537,297	2,738,863	140,462,105
17,272,112	11,881,416	1,451,691	2,650,754	46,505,530
14,025,505	10,157,415	1,193,764	2,027,798	36,362,426
45.79	72.51	77.65	74.04	25.89
81.20	85.49	82.23	76.50	78.19
127,173,272	122,119,547	19,521,612	42,883,844	380,676,165
4,150	8,720	12,700	15,660	2,710
7,360	10,280	13,450	16,180	8,190
9,070	12,020	16,350	21,150	10,470
11.59	16.34	21.72	27.37	17.33
14,739,119	19,950,535	4,239,460	11,736,078	56,041,831
481	1,424	2,758	4,285	470

in the top 35 percent accounted for 82 percent of the reduction in taxable income (see table 6.2).[21]

However, these measurements of taxable income understate the realized benefit of the deduction to higher-income households. Because higher-income taxpayers pay a higher marginal rate on their taxable income, any deduction that decreases taxable income is more valuable to a high-income taxpayer than to a low-income taxpayer. Looking at the aggregate effective tax break for low-income households compared to high-income households, one finds that the 2 percent of income earners who make more than $250,000 annually receive nearly 25 times more from the MID than those who earn less than $15,000 (see table 6.2).

Looking at average effective tax breaks per return, one discovers that the difference between income brackets is even greater because less than 3 percent of households earning $15,000 or less claim the MID. The average effective tax reduction for each return among the lowest-income families is $14. Compare that to the average $4,285 tax reduction for tax filers who earn $250,000 or more. The large variation in nominal benefits is one reason that many economists consider the MID to be a regressive tax policy. High-income earners receive an average tax benefit that is nine times greater than that of tax filers earning $50,000 to $100,000 (see table 6.2). The effective tax reduction of the MID per return for tax filers earning $100,000 to $200,000 is $1,424, which is nearly 10 times the $147 saved by taxpayers earning $30,000 to $50,000.

In terms of effective tax reduction, taxpayers earning more than $100,000 (13 percent of tax returns) receive more than $35 billion in tax reductions, whereas taxpayers earning less than $50,000 (65 percent of tax returns) receive a little more than $5 billion. Less than 20 percent of all income tax returns that report less than $40,000 in earnings claim the MID, whereas approximately 75 percent of income tax returns with reported earnings of $100,000 to $1 million claim the MID (see table 6.3). Because of the extreme differences in who benefits from the MID, many scholars believe that it is highly skewed toward high-income households.[22]

In addition to favoring higher-income earners, the benefits associated with the MID favor particular geographic locations. According to economists Todd Sinai and Joseph Gyourko's study on tax-favored housing for the years 1980–2000, the biggest benefits went, in descending order, to Washington, DC; Hawaii; California; New York; Massachusetts; Connecticut; and New Jersey—5 of which are among the top 14 median state incomes.[23] Owner-occupied benefits exceeded $8,000 in each of these high-income states, which also have the highest state marginal tax rates. In another study, Gyourko and Sinai find that three metropolitan areas—New York–northern New Jersey, Los Angeles–Riverside–Orange County, and San Francisco–Oakland–San Jose—received 5 percent of net positive benefits from the MID.[24]

MID state tax policies suffer from equity and efficiency problems similar to those of federal tax policy. As Richard Green and Andrew Reschovsky

Table 6.3. Share of Taxpayers Claiming the Mortgage Interest Deduction in 2010, by Income Range

ADJUSTED GROSS INCOME RANGE ($)	SHARE WHO ITEMIZE MORTGAGE INTEREST DEDUCTION (%)
All	25.86
0–4,999	1.97
5,000–9,999	2.77
10,000–14,999	3.85
15,000–19,999	5.78
20,000–24,999	8.02
25,000–29,999	11.45
30,000–39,999	17.80
40,000–49,999	27.38
50,000–74,999	40.45
75,000–99,999	56.21
100,000–199,999	73.28
200,000–249,999	78.63
250,000–499,999	77.54
500,000–999,999	72.64
1,000,000–1,499,999	66.37
1,500,000–1,999,999	64.57
2,000,000–4,999,999	60.98
5,000,000–9,999,999	53.99
10,000,000 and above	47.39

Source: Data from the Statistics of Income Division of the Internal Revenue Service.

explain, "In 33 of the 42 states with individual income taxes, mortgage interest is deductible in the calculation of state income tax liabilities, further increasing the tax subsidy to homeownership."[25] In fact, all states with an MID (except Alabama) favor high-income households relative to middle-income households.[26] Table 6.4 shows a state-by-state comparison of the percentage point reduction in effective tax rates among households with $50,000 in earnings and those with $200,000 in earnings that claim a state MID. The table also provides a ranking of the difference in effective tax rate reduction by state. These data suggest that state MIDs offer a more significant decrease in effective tax rates for high-income earners than for middle-income households. Thus, the economic distortions caused by the state MIDs, and their regressive effects, go even beyond those at the federal level.

The demographics of the main beneficiaries of the MID are more particular than just income and geography. Because the MID is something that is used over an extended period of time, MID users who recently purchased a home have a particularly strong interest in continuation of the MID in the tax code. Young, high-earner homeowners would be the most disadvantaged by its repeal.[27] Evidence also suggests that two-earner households would be particularly affected by changes to the MID, because they tend to use greater amounts of debt to finance their homes.[28]

The MID thus frequently gives higher-income taxpayers a tax deduction for a purchase that they would have made anyway.[29] Glaeser and Shapiro conclude that the MID does little to increase the country's

Table 6.4. State Mortgage Interest Deduction Favors High-Income Earners, 2010

STATE	STATE MID?	$50,000 ADJUSTED GROSS INCOME		$200,000 ADJUSTED GROSS INCOME		DIFFERENCE	
		EFFECTIVE STATE TAX BENEFIT AS % OF INCOME	EFFECTIVE TAX BENEFIT AS % OF INTEREST EXPENSE	EFFECTIVE STATE TAX BENEFIT AS % OF INCOME	EFFECTIVE TAX BENEFIT AS % OF INTEREST EXPENSE	EFFECTIVE STATE TAX BENEFIT AS % OF INCOME	EFFECTIVE TAX BENEFIT AS % OF INTEREST EXPENSE
North Carolina	Yes	0.03	0.00	0.55	5.45	-0.52	-5.45
Missouri	Yes	0.00	0.00	0.46	5.35	-0.46	-5.35
Arkansas	Yes	0.00	0.00	0.43	5.29	-0.43	-5.29
California	Yes	0.24	1.97	1.05	7.17	-0.81	-5.20
Georgia	Yes	0.00	0.00	0.55	5.16	-0.55	-5.16
Wisconsin	Yes	0.00	0.00	0.41	5.00	-0.41	-5.00
Virginia	Yes	0.00	0.00	0.50	4.28	-0.50	-4.28

Iowa	Yes	0.38	1.99	0.43	6.13	−0.05	−4.14
Kansas	Yes	0.00	0.00	0.31	3.97	−0.31	−3.97
Maryland	Yes	0.00	0.00	0.45	3.92	−0.45	−3.92
Maine	Yes	0.00	0.00	0.29	3.51	−0.29	−3.51
Montana	Yes	0.19	0.37	0.34	3.81	−0.15	−3.44
Minnesota	Yes	0.00	0.00	0.33	3.32	−0.33	−3.32
Idaho	Yes	0.00	0.00	0.32	3.27	−0.32	−3.27
South Carolina	Yes	0.00	0.00	0.32	3.13	−0.32	−3.13
Rhode Island	Yes	0.00	0.00	0.27	3.07	−0.27	−3.07
Delaware	Yes	0.54	1.69	0.46	4.65	0.08	−2.96
Arizona	Yes	0.06	0.16	0.32	2.63	−0.26	−2.47
Colorado	Yes	0.00	0.00	0.25	2.26	−0.25	−2.26
New York	Yes	0.00	0.00	0.25	2.22	−0.25	−2.22
Oregon	Yes	0.99	5.28	0.78	7.35	0.21	−2.07
Mississippi	Yes	0.32	1.48	0.28	3.54	0.04	−2.06

(continued)

Table 6.4. (continued)

| STATE | STATE MID? | $50,000 ADJUSTED GROSS INCOME | | $200,000 ADJUSTED GROSS INCOME | | DIFFERENCE | |
		EFFECTIVE STATE TAX BENEFIT AS % OF INCOME	EFFECTIVE TAX BENEFIT AS % OF INTEREST EXPENSE	EFFECTIVE STATE TAX BENEFIT AS % OF INCOME	EFFECTIVE TAX BENEFIT AS % OF INTEREST EXPENSE	EFFECTIVE STATE TAX BENEFIT AS % OF INCOME	EFFECTIVE TAX BENEFIT AS % OF INTEREST EXPENSE
Hawaii	Yes	1.35	4.96	0.90	6.96	0.45	-2.00
Vermont	Yes	0.00	0.00	0.15	1.97	-0.15	-1.97
New Mexico	Yes	0.00	0.00	0.18	1.89	-0.18	-1.89
Nebraska	Yes	0.00	0.00	0.11	1.48	-0.11	-1.48
Kentucky	Yes	0.50	3.83	0.41	5.17	0.09	-1.34
Oklahoma	Yes	0.00	0.00	0.10	1.32	-0.10	-1.32
Louisiana	Yes	0.00	0.00	0.09	1.15	-0.09	-1.15

		0.00	0.00	0.00	0.03	0.50	-0.03	-0.50
North Dakota	Yes	0.00	0.00	0.00	0.00	0.00	0.00	-0.50
Alaska	No	0.00	0.00	0.00	0.00	0.00	0.00	0.00
Connecticut	No	0.00	0.00	0.00	0.00	0.00	0.00	0.00
Florida	No	0.00	0.00	0.00	0.00	0.00	0.00	0.00
Illinois	No	0.00	0.00	0.00	0.00	0.00	0.00	0.00
Indiana	No	0.00	0.00	0.00	0.00	0.00	0.00	0.00
Massachusetts	No	0.00	0.00	0.00	0.00	0.00	0.00	0.00
Michigan	No	0.00	0.00	0.00	0.00	0.00	0.00	0.00
Nevada	No	0.00	0.00	0.00	0.00	0.00	0.00	0.00
New Hampshire	No	0.00	0.00	0.00	0.00	0.00	0.00	0.00
New Jersey	No	0.00	0.00	0.00	0.00	0.00	0.00	0.00
Ohio	No	0.00	0.00	0.00	0.00	0.00	0.00	0.00
Pennsylvania	No	0.00	0.00	0.00	0.00	0.00	0.00	0.00
South Dakota	No	0.00	0.00	0.00	0.00	0.00	0.00	0.00
Tennessee	No	0.00	0.00	0.00	0.00	0.00	0.00	0.00

(continued)

Table 6.4. (*continued*)

STATE	STATE MID?	$50,000 ADJUSTED GROSS INCOME		$200,000 ADJUSTED GROSS INCOME		DIFFERENCE	
		EFFECTIVE STATE TAX BENEFIT AS % OF INCOME	EFFECTIVE TAX BENEFIT AS % OF INTEREST EXPENSE	EFFECTIVE STATE TAX BENEFIT AS % OF INCOME	EFFECTIVE TAX BENEFIT AS % OF INTEREST EXPENSE	EFFECTIVE STATE TAX BENEFIT AS % OF INCOME	EFFECTIVE TAX BENEFIT AS % OF INTEREST EXPENSE
Texas	No	0.00	0.00	0.00	0.00	0.00	0.00
Utah	No	0.00	0.00	0.00	0.00	0.00	0.00
Washington	No	0.00	0.00	0.00	0.00	0.00	0.00
West Virginia	No	0.00	0.00	0.00	0.00	0.00	0.00
Wyoming	No	0.00	0.00	0.00	0.00	0.00	0.00
Alabama	Yes	0.68	4.89	0.41	4.46	0.27	0.43

Source: Authors' calculations and data from Donald Morris and Jing Wang, "How and Why States Use the Home Mortgage Interest Deduction," *Tax Notes* 64 (June 4, 2012): 697–713.

homeownership rate; rather it increases the demand for debt and modifies the progressivity of the tax code.[30] A similar conclusion was reached by Thomas Boehm and Alan Schlottmann, who find that across the 1970s and through the 1990s, the MID increased demand for housing by 2.6 to 3.5 percentage points but that the MID may have had greater influence in the 1970s and 1980s because of an increased likelihood that a given person was a homeowner in the 1990s.[31]

An effective federal tax policy that promotes home-ownership should ensure that any tax benefit goes to households at the margin—those that would not necessarily purchase a home without the tax benefit. As long as housing tax policy exists, it should be designed to encourage access to the social benefits among potential homeowners who would not otherwise buy a home. Some of these social benefits are discussed in the next section.

SOCIAL BENEFITS AND COSTS OF HOMEOWNERSHIP

The social benefits discussed in this section are a summary of research on the positive and negative externalities associated with homeownership. To the extent that the MID increases homeownership rates, these issues are influenced by tax policy as well (see table 6.5).

Positive externalities from homeownership may include benefits to the next generation as well as better property maintenance and stronger communities. In their 1997 study, economists Richard Green and

Table 6.5. Positive and Negative Externalities of Homeownership

TYPE	SOCIAL OUTCOME AND SUPPORTING RESEARCH
Positive externalities	
Better property maintenance	Rental homes depreciate at a faster rate than owner-occupied single-family homes (DiPasquale and Glaeser 1999; Shilling, Sirmans, and Dombrow 1991; Galster 1983).
More pleasant community	A significant amount of spending in expensive areas of the country is on land or community amenities (Glaeser and Gyourko 2001).
	Homeowners are more likely to make political choices that favor the long-run health of their community (as measured by school funding and road maintenance). Municipalities with a higher level of renters, who have an incentive to favor policies with short-run gains, vote for policies favoring social welfare and hospitals (DiPasquale and Glaeser 1999; Monroe 2001).
	Homeowners are more likely to invest in communities because of the high cost of moving (DiPasquale and Glaeser 1999; Monroe 2001).
More politically informed residents	Homeowners are more likely to be informed about political figures and to be active in local politics (Glaeser and Shapiro 2003).
More successful children	Children of homeowners are 9 percent less likely to drop out of school than children of comparable renters (Green and White 1997).
Negative externalities	
More unemployment	Higher homeownership rates lead to high levels of unemployment. Areas with renters can move more quickly in response to an economic shock (Oswald 1999).

(*continued*)

Table 6.5. (*continued*)

TYPE	SOCIAL OUTCOME AND SUPPORTING RESEARCH
More income segregation	Encouraging more housing consumption encourages wealthier people to leave small city apartments for larger homes on the fringe of the city, thereby imposing negative social costs on people remaining in the city and increasing segregation by income (Voith 1999).
	Homeownership can cause political behavior that restricts the supply of new housing via zoning and other land-use controls in order to raise prices (Glaeser and Shapiro 2003).

Sources: Edward L. Glaeser and Jesse M. Shapiro, "The Benefits of the Home Mortgage Interest Deduction," in *Tax Policy and the Economy*, vol. 17, ed. James M. Poterba (Cambridge, MA: MIT Press, 2003), 37–82; Denise DiPasquale and Edward L. Glaeser, "Incentives and Social Capital: Are Homeowners Better Citizens?," *Journal of Urban Economics* 45, no. 2 (March 1999): 354–84; James Shilling, C. F. Sirmans, and Jonathan Dombrow, "Measuring Depreciation in Single-Family Rental and Owner-Occupied Housing," *Journal of Housing Economics* 1, no. 4 (December 1991): 368–83; George Galster, "Empirical Evidence on Cross-Tenure Differences in House Maintenance and Conditions," *Land Economics* 59, no. 1 (February 1983): 107–13; Edward L. Glaeser and Joseph Gyourko, "Urban Decline and Durable Housing," NBER Working Paper 8598, National Bureau of Economic Research, Cambridge, MA, November 2001; Albert Monroe, "The Effects of Homeownership on Communities" (PhD diss., Harvard University, May 2001); Richard Green and Michelle White, "Measuring the Benefits of Homeowning: Effects on Children," *Journal of Urban Economics* 41, no. 3 (May 1997): 441–461; Andrew J. Oswald, "The Housing Market and Europe's Unemployment: A Non-technical Paper," Working Paper, University of Warwick, Coventry, UK, 1999; Richard Voith, "Does the Federal Tax Treatment of Housing Affect the Pattern of Metropolitan Development?," *Federal Reserve Bank of Philadelphia Business Review*, March–April 1999, 3–16.

Michelle White find that children of homeowners were 9 percent more likely to stay in school than the children of renters.[32] Green and White monetized the value of a low-income renter becoming a homeowner at $31,000.[33] Economists Glaeser and Shapiro also find evidence that homeowners take better care of their property and tend to work harder at making their community more pleasant. Homeowners tend to be more interested in their community because of high mobility costs and because the value of their asset is tied to the quality of their community.[34] These fixed interests also lead homeowners to be more involved politically.

Greater political activity around a set of concentrated interests also can produce negative externalities. According to Richard Voith, former economist at the Federal Reserve Bank of Philadelphia, the MID promotes zoning laws that increase neighborhood gentrification. For example, a zoning law that mandates a minimum lot size works in favor of high-income households and against low-income households, making lot purchases cost prohibitive for some low-income households. Hence, larger suburban plots attract higher-income households, whereas low-income households are concentrated in older, denser urban neighborhoods.[35] Gentrification can have significant implications for the provision of certain public goods and for public school systems.

Other authors, including Henry Aaron, Harvey Rosen, Kenneth Rosen, James Poterba, and Edwin Mills, have examined the social costs associated with the MID.[36] This chapter does not attempt to conclude whether the externalities from homeownership are a net social gain or loss. But it seems likely that the effect of any positive externalities from homeownership would be relatively greater for low-income taxpayers than for high-income taxpayers.

ECONOMICS OF THE MORTGAGE INTEREST DEDUCTION

In addition to the social effects of the MID, it has economic and public policy implications. One of the main objections to the MID is that preferential housing encourages overinvestment in housing. Although the MID has little effect on the homeownership rate, it does have a significant role in increasing the amount of debt and the size of a home that is purchased. Studies estimate that the MID encourages people to acquire homes that are 10 to 20 percent larger than they would have purchased without the MID.[37]

Such investment occurs at the expense of investments in plants and equipment.[38] Money should be invested at the most economically efficient point. Tax deductions create an artificially low hurdle for investment dollars. The healthiest economy is one in which the most valued investments are not discouraged in place of government-favored alternatives.

Taxpayers reshuffle their investment portfolios in response to changes in the tax code. For example, when the Tax Reform Act of 1986 ended the deductibility of consumer debt, high-income taxpayers increased their consumption of the MID. Economists Jonathan Skinner and Daniel Feenberg found that high-income earners increased their consumption of interest on housing by 67 to 86 cents for every dollar decrease in consumer interest paid.[39] Dean Maki draws similar conclusions.[40]

Another important implication of the Skinner and Feenberg study is that estimates about revenue lost from the MID overstate the true loss in government revenue. Taxpayers adjust their behavior in response to changes in tax-preferred investments in an effort to minimize their tax burden. These behavioral responses reduce the tax revenue that could be expected to be gained by ending any given tax expenditure. First, revenue may be lower than anticipated because taxpayers may transfer some investments into a different form of tax-preferred investment. Second, if mortgage interest were no longer a tax-preferred investment, taxpayers would draw down on holdings of interest, dividends, and capital gains to reduce their principal and interest payments. Because other forms of taxable income would be used to lower outstanding debt, there would be less government revenue from taxing those alternative forms of investment.[41] As a result, estimates of what portion of the MID would be collected as revenue in the provision's absence vary: James Follain and Lisa Sturman Melamed estimate 25 percent; Martin Gervais and Manish Pandey estimate 58 percent; William Gale, Jonathan Gruber, and Seth Stephens-Davidowitz estimate 84 percent; and James Poterba and Todd Sinai estimate 80 percent.[42] Therefore, even if the MID were eliminated, it would not lead to an instant $69 billion in annual tax revenue for the US Treasury.[43]

Last, the MID increases the demand for housing, thus increasing both the price of homes and interest rates. Estimates of how much the MID increases housing prices range from 10 to 15 percent.[44] Lawrence Yun, chief economist for the National Association of Realtors, claims that eliminating the MID would result in trillions of dollars of wealth destruction and uncertainty.[45] One study finds that the increase in housing prices is largely driven by the demand for homes that are 10 to 20 percent larger than the homes buyers would choose in the absence of the MID.[46] Marquette University economist Andrew Hanson estimates that the MID increases home sizes by as much as 1,400 square feet.[47] A rise in homeownership rates further increases local prices, perhaps by as much as a 1.5 percent for every 1 percent increase in homeownership.[48] And because the MID increases the demand for debt, banks lend money at higher interest rates. Hanson estimates that 9 to 17 percent of the MID subsidy is offset by higher interest rates.[49]

PAST REFORMS AND POLICY OPTIONS

The Tax Reform Act of 1986 significantly reduced the value of the MID by reducing marginal tax rates and increasing the standard deduction. James Follain and David Ling estimate that the deadweight economic loss of housing subsidies was decreased by one-third as a result of the lower marginal tax rates mandated in the act.[50] The lower tax rates significantly diminished use of the MID by lower-income households, although the reduction in use was not quite as great as for high-income households. Furthermore, increases in the standard deduction made it less desirable or unnecessary for low-income households to claim itemized deductions, thus sparing these taxpayers associated tax complexities. Follain and Ling report that in 1991 the interest deduction became "essentially worthless" for a household with a typical loan–to–market value ratio and an annual income below $42,500.[51] In inflation-adjusted terms, this amount would be nearly $73,000 in 2014.[52] Consistent with other data, there seems to be an increase in homeownership and in the use of the MID beginning around this income level (see tables 6.2 and 6.3, pages 136 and 140).

In light of the regressive nature of the MID's benefit distribution and the lack of desired policy outcomes, there are reforms to housing tax policy that could more effectively help the intended beneficiaries. Many of these policy changes might not—and likely would not—solve many of the economic and investment inefficiencies that a housing subsidy creates. Before moving on to policy recommendations, we describe three alternative reforms considered by others in the literature: (a) refundable and nonrefundable tax credits on mortgage interest, (b) a fixed tax credit for homeownership, and (c) a one-time home-buyer credit.

One of the first options addressed in the literature is a refundable tax credit for mortgage interest payments. Green and Reschovsky estimate that a credit equal to 21 percent of mortgage interest payments would raise total homeownership by 3 percent. Households earning less than an estimated inflation-adjusted

$145,000 ($100,000 in 1997) would experience an increase in homeownership, whereas the wealthiest households would experience less than a 1 percent decrease.[53] These changes in homeownership rates from the simulation models run by Green and Reschovsky imply that nearly 3.1 million households would become homeowners, while only about 30,000 high-income homeowners would choose to become renters.[54] The refundable tax credit could lower tax liabilities to below zero for many homeowners with mortgage interest.

In 2010, the National Commission on Fiscal Responsibility and Reform (otherwise known as the Simpson–Bowles Commission) suggested reforming the MID into a nonrefundable tax credit for mortgage interest. Nonrefundable tax credits can lower tax liabilities down to zero but not below. The commission proposed imposing a 12 percent tax credit cap on interest paid and lowering the maximum qualifying debt from $1 million to $500,000.[55] Changing the cap would significantly scale back housing tax subsidies to high-income earners because only 0.39 percent of mortgages exceed the current $1 million cap.[56] The commission also revisited one of the policy ideas of the 2005 President's Advisory Panel on Federal Tax Reform. The panel had considered reforming the MID into a credit on 15 percent of eligible mortgage interest to encourage homeownership in general, not just the purchase of bigger homes.[57] The ceiling on eligible mortgage principal would have been limited to between $227,000 and $412,000 (approximately $272,000 and $493,000, adjusted for inflation), depending on average regional housing costs. Economists David Ling and Gary McGill examine a 15 percent credit in their 2007 paper. Without accounting for behavioral effects, they find that the credit would decrease tax liabilities for low-income households, whereas some households earning in excess of $75,000 would see their tax burdens rise.[58] In an earlier paper, James Follain, David Ling, and Gary McGill petition for the introduction of a flat nonrefundable tax credit.[59] Amanda Eng, Harvey Galper, Georgia Ivsin, and Eric Toder present two different proposals for a nonrefundable credit of 15 percent and 20 percent, respectively, of eligible mortgage interest to replace the existing MID.[60] These two policy proposals offer a good starting place for reform, but setting the tax credit at a specific value could be a simpler and more effective way to encourage low-income homeownership.

A second option for reform is an annual tax credit for owning a home. Adam Carasso, Eugene Steuerle, and Elizabeth Bell examine a 1.03 percent credit, in 2005, based on a home purchase price of up to $100,000 (an inflation-adjusted $119,000)—regardless of whether a mortgage is held. According to their analysis, households in the bottom four quintiles would experience a decrease in taxes, whereas the top quintile would experience a tax increase of 2.5 percent.[61] Similarly, politics professor Peter Dreier argues for a complete substitution of the MID for a housing credit.[62] The proposal is interesting, but Dreier does not estimate how the proposal would affect housing demand.

A third potential reform discussed in the literature is replacement of the MID with a one-time home-buyer credit on a first home. According to Richard Green and Kerry Vandell, this subsidy would be approximately $33,000 for the 2 million people annually who are first-time home buyers.[63] David Ling and Gary McGill claim that the first-time home-buyer credit would have a particularly strong effect on promoting homeowner-ship among low-income households.[64] However, economists Matthew Chambers, Carlos Garriga, and Don Schlagenhauf find that the one-time credit actu-ally backfires on the intent of increasing aggregate homeownership levels.[65] According to their research, the effects of the credit on home prices, in addition to offsetting increases in marginal rates, actually decrease the aggregate homeownership rate among young and poorer households. However, these authors examined only the effect of the credit on renters with offsetting increases in marginal rates without account-ing for conversion of the MID into a credit.

All these policy options provide a starting place for a discussion about reforming the MID. However, none would be as effective as the policy recommen-dations proposed here in terms of creating economic efficiency and tax code simplicity, as well as encourag-ing homeownership.

CONCLUSION

Two policy recommendations are made here—one based on tax policy principles and one on improv-ing homeownership rates. The first-best option is to eliminate the MID.[66] Only a full repeal of tax-favorable housing policies in exchange for lower marginal rates will eliminate economic inefficiencies. Economists often point out that lower marginal tax rates in general improve economic efficiency and decrease deadweight loss.

The strength of eliminating the MID is that it would reduce the economic distortions of subsidized housing for higher-income households. Eliminating the MID may slightly decrease the demand for housing among some low-income households that actually have sufficient mortgage interest to itemize. But this decrease seems relatively small, given that the MID is used so infrequently by low-income households,[67] and the bulk of the decrease in the demand for mortgage debt would come from households with large loans that exceed the loan limits of Fannie Mae and Freddie Mac.[68] However, James Poterba and Todd Sinai estimate that, in the event of abolishment of the MID, the few low-income households that now use it would be disproportionately taxed compared to higher-income users.[69] These progressivity concerns would likely be addressed to some degree if lower marginal tax rates or a higher standard deduction were instituted to keep the reform revenue neutral. A cleaner federal tax code would move away from the current tax-driven overvaluation of the housing industry. Eliminating the MID would encourage the purchase of more moderately sized homes, because the existing tax subsidy encourages the purchase of homes that are 10 to 20 percent larger than would otherwise be purchased, predominantly among high-income households.[70] Revenue-neutral tax reform that eliminated the bias toward homeownership would encourage higher-income households to shift some housing investments to more socially productive investments.

A second-best alternative tax reform proposed here is to grant a fixed $900 credit for having a mortgage.[71] Green and Reschovsky consider this form of tax credit in their 1997 paper. They claim that a fixed $850 credit (approximately $1,250 adjusted for inflation for 2014) would increase the homeownership rate by 5.3 percent.[72] Similarly, a revenue-neutral fixed credit of $903 can be estimated by using the most recent tax and housing data, before accounting for behavioral effects.[73] The credit could be granted for a specific number of years for an owner-occupied home. Its fixed property might reduce tax code complexity and would not be weighted toward greater debt financing. The credit should also be adjusted periodically to account for inflation and, if simplicity is desired, rounded up to the nearest $50 or $100. For example, a credit estimated at $903 could be rounded up to $950.

Policymakers should continue to take steps toward greater simplicity and efficiency in the US tax code by lowering tax rates and increasing the standard deduction. A cleaner tax code would bring more equality to investment opportunities and would be a step toward greater tax fairness for renters and homeowners with the same incomes.[74] But given the difficulties of eliminating the MID outright, including the special-interest groups that would oppose any such elimination, tax-favored housing should, at a minimum, promote homeownership, not necessarily larger and more expensive homes or second homes used as vacation properties. A fixed nonrefundable tax credit of approximately $900 for a primary mortgage offers the most effective means of both increasing homeownership and properly aligning the purported policy goals of the MID with desired outcomes.

CHAPTER 7

How Do People Respond to the Marriage Tax Penalty?

P oliticians often stress that marriage is a key institution that promotes strong family values. However, some aspects of the federal tax code do not promote marriage. Because of the structure of joint income tax filing, many couples face significant tax disincentives to marriage. The United States is one of only seven countries in the Organisation for Economic Co-operation and Development that uses joint taxation for married couples.[1] This chapter uses the term *marriage tax penalty* to refer to the disadvantageous tax treatment of a married couple's joint income relative to two individuals earning an equivalent income but choosing cohabitation over marriage.[2] Economists Daniel Feenberg and Harvey Rosen note that for some low-income couples in 1990, "The size of the marriage tax is now quite extraordinary, amounting to over 18 percent of total income."[3] Many of the issues surrounding the marriage tax penalty remain unchanged. Given the generally more elastic labor supply of married women, the marriage tax penalty may give married women in all income ranges incentive not to work outside the home.[4] In 1942, feminist activist Florence Guy Seabury sent a letter to the *New*

York Times regarding a proposal at that time for joint income taxation in which she wrote:

> To those who know the long struggle of women in this country to own property, to control their earnings, to be guardians of their children, to move out of the subject class, this measure is a symbol. It represents the defeat of a major principle of our way of life.[5]

Certainly, in 1942, wide disparity existed between male and female labor force participation rates and wages. Today, with increasingly more equivalent wages between men and women and a record number of women working, reducing the marriage tax penalty makes more sense than ever.[6]

Not all joint filers incur a penalty in the federal tax code, however. Some receive a marriage bonus, which is the advantageous tax treatment of a married couple's combined income relative to two individual filers earning an equivalent combined income. The marriage bonus most commonly occurs with single-earner households. The marriage tax penalty most commonly occurs with two-earner households. For the couples most burdened by the marriage tax penalty, it acts as a financial disincentive to marriage.[7]

The penalty is predominantly borne by two groups of two-earner couples: (a) low-income, two-earner households filing for the earned income tax credit (EITC) and (b) low- and middle-income, two-earner couples for which the two salaries are roughly equal. The effect of marriage tax penalty is greatest for low-income households that use the EITC,[8] the same households that would potentially benefit most from the acclaimed social benefits of marriage.[9]

Where the marriage bonus is present, it discourages labor force participation by secondary earners, who are predominantly women. A higher marginal tax rate for a single-earner household more strongly depresses the economic return of a potential secondary earner. On their own and not married, secondary earners could experience an entry marginal tax rate of 10 percent rather than a rate of 25 percent or higher. As a result, economic growth and productivity are lost as a consequence of the filing status requirements applying to married couples. An ideal tax code would be neutral with respect to marriage.

EFFECT OF THE MARRIAGE TAX PENALTY ON EXISTING MARRIAGES

No marriage penalty or tax per se appears in the US tax code. The penalty phenomenon emerges as an economic effect of joint taxation on the combined incomes of two married earners. Williams College economist Sara LaLumia examines the historical effect of joint taxation:

> Joint taxation equalizes the marginal tax rates of a husband and wife. Because husbands tended to earn more than wives, the introduction of joint taxation lowered husbands' marginal tax rates and raised wives' marginal tax rates, on average.[10]

When most households contained only one working spouse, joint taxation did not result in a tax penalty for the majority of married couples. Traditionally, men were the breadwinners, and women raised children and managed the home. As the proportion of women in the labor force increased dramatically from 1960 to 2000 and as women's wages rose, the marriage tax penalty became an increasingly common issue for two-earner marriages. Economists Michael Bar and Oksana Leukhina write about the rise in female labor force participation during the 40 years from 1960 to 2000: "The proportion of two-earner couples among married couples of working age in the U.S. rose from 34% to 77%."[11] With the increased number of two-earner married couples, the existing tax code plays a prominent role in discouraging earned income by a secondary earner because the secondary earner's first dollar is often taxed at a higher rate. The marginal tax rates are then significantly distorted by factors such as the EITC, the tax code's treatment of the earned income difference for a two-earner married couple, and family size.

Low-income couples in the joint income salary range of $30,000 to $50,000 face particularly strong tax disincentives to marriage.[12] As a percentage of income, the marriage penalty is highest for couples in that income range because the EITC is phased out for both earners.[13] A substantial package of transfer benefits for having dependent children can create strong financial incentives for divorce among married joint filers and continued cohabitation among single filers.[14]

Tax law generates significant horizontal inequalities that are based on each earner's income and how many dependent children a household has. Horizontal inequality means identically sized families earning the same amount of income are taxed differently. Joint income filing penalizes marriage when both spouses earn a similar amount of income.[15] For example, the tax code subsidizes single-worker households earning $60,000 but penalizes two-worker households earning the same amount when the income earners are married (see table 7.1).

For those qualifying for the EITC, horizontal inequality has historically depended on family size, where having one or more dependent children actually penalizes two-earner married couples. Examining the marriage tax penalty over 14 years, economists Nada Eissa and Hilary Hoynes find the following:

> Penalized married taxpayers with less than $20,000 earned income face an average marriage penalty of 8 percent of income. . . . [M]arriage tax penalties increase with family size (number of children) among EITC-eligible couples. . . . [A] dual-earning couple with two children faces a sizeable marriage tax penalty of $2,733 (11.4 percent of income). A similar childless couple, on the other hand, faces a tax penalty of $210 (1 percent of income).[16]

Benefits can also arise. In a 1995 paper, Feenberg and Rosen find that 52 percent of American families

Table 7.1. Effects of Various Proposals on Tax Liability of Couples

	50-50 EARNINGS: $30,000 AND $30,000	100-0 EARNINGS: $60,000 AND $0	50-50 EARNINGS: $150,000 AND $150,000	100-0 EARNINGS: $300,000 AND $0
Current law				
Aggregate liability of single, unmarried couple	$2,524	$6,319	$50,685	$61,649
Joint liability of married couple	$3,048	$3,048	$54,298	$54,298
Penalty/(bonus)	$524	($3,241)	$4,243	($7,351)
Horizontal equality	No	No	No	No
Effect on secondary earner labor participation	Neutral	Negative	Neutral	Negative
Mandatory single filing				
Aggregate liability of single, unmarried couple	$3,048	$5,331	$53,020	$65,584
Joint liability of married couple	$3,048	$5,331	$53,020	$65,584

Penalty/(bonus)	$0	$0	$0	$0
Horizontal equality	Yes	Yes	Yes	Yes
Effect on secondary earner labor participation	Neutral	Neutral	Neutral	Neutral
50–50 income splitting[a]				
Aggregate liability of single, unmarried couple	$3,048	$5,331	$53,020	$65,584
Joint liability of married couple	$3,048	$5,331	$53,020	$53,020
Penalty/(bonus)	$0	$0	$0	$12,564
Horizontal equality	Yes	Yes	Yes	Yes
Effect on secondary earner labor participation	Neutral	Unknown	Neutral	Unknown

Source: Authors' calculations using IRS rates for 2014.

Note: Table assumes couples earning $60,000 claim the standard deduction and that couples earning $150,000 claim itemized deductions equal to 18 percent of their adjusted gross income when filing single and when filing jointly.

a. Under 50–50 income splitting, most of the defined joint filing brackets are twice the width of single-filer brackets. The joint filing bracket narrows progressively on reaching the tail end of the 25 percent bracket. A pure income-splitting reform would not incorporate this progressivity, thereby reducing the marriage penalty.

paid a marriage tax penalty and 38 percent received a marriage tax bonus.[17] Today, such inequities still exist and will continue as long as filing on the basis of marital status is required.

MARRIAGE INCENTIVES

Expansions of the EITC under the Tax Reform Act of 1986, the Omnibus Budget Reconciliation Act of 1990, and the Omnibus Budget Reconciliation Act of 1993 reduced the marriage tax penalty for low-income couples.[18] Eissa and Hoynes find a steady decrease in the penalty from the 1980s into the late 1990s: "Each of three tax acts passed between 1984 and 1997 reduced the marriage tax cost for the poorest families, so that marriage cost was about $450 lower in 1997 compared to 1984."[19] These acts also expanded benefits to single filers. Although these reforms did reduce the federal income tax costs associated with marriage, they did not do so relative to the alternative of cohabitation. As a result, marriage is not a financially neutral choice for many couples. Economists Leslie Whittington and James Alm come to a similar conclusion: "A tax plan that gives larger reductions to single individuals can actually increase the marriage penalty. In short, reducing marriage penalties is not as simple as reducing income taxes."[20]

The 2001 and 2003 tax reforms passed under President George W. Bush are illustrative.[21] These reforms were intended to reduce the tax penalty associated with marriage by reintroducing a two-earner deduction of 10 percent on the earnings of a lower-income spouse, up to an annual income of $30,000.[22] The deduction thus allowed a $3,000 maximum subtraction from income subject to federal taxation. In 2003, the White House justified the deduction as follows:

> Couples frequently face a higher tax burden after they marry. High marginal tax rates act as a tollgate, limiting the access of low and moderate income earners to the middle class. The current tax code frequently taxes couples more after they get married. This marriage tax contradicts our values and any reasonable sense of fairness.[23]

Although these reforms decreased the negative tax consequences of marriage, they did not account for the effect on the alternative to marriage: cohabitation. Although the marriage tax penalty decreased, the tax benefits of cohabitation increased at a faster rate. Whittington and Alm examine a few scenarios for a couple with $60,000 in annual earnings and find that, "although the Bush tax plan lowers the liabilities of both singles and married couples, the plan lowers taxes more for singles than for married couples."[24] Hence, although they were intended to create income tax incentives that favor married-couple family structures, the reforms actually may encourage greater cohabitation. Whittington and Alm call this "a result that seems counter to the family-oriented image favored by President Bush."[25]

On a more positive note, a 2010 study by Hayley Fisher finds that individuals with the least education were four times more responsive to the financial incentives of marriage than individuals with the most education.[26] These data suggest that public policies meant to increase the financial benefits of marriage without increasing a single filer's tax liability might be more successful at promoting marriage than previously thought. Marriage neutrality in the tax code could be successful in promoting marriage among low-income taxpayers.

DIVORCE INCENTIVES

One of the consequences of the implicit marriage tax penalty is that it increases the probability of divorce for certain income ranges. Economist Stacy Dickert-Conlin finds that "most low-income couples are eligible for higher welfare benefits if they are separated rather than married."[27] Lower tax liability outside of marriage is positively correlated with the decision to divorce at statistically significant levels.[28] Using 1990 data, Dickert-Conlin finds that the marriage tax penalty has the strongest effects at the tail ends of income distribution:

> The family at the 10th percentile in the distribution of the marriage tax penalty faces a $3,067 marriage tax subsidy. A 50 percent reduction in the subsidy is correlated with a 10.8 percent increase in the probability of separating. . . . At the 90th percentile in the distribution of the marriage tax penalty, the family faces a marriage tax penalty of $1,285.[29]

Lowering the marriage tax penalty for families in the 90th percentile in the distribution of the penalty by 50 percent would decrease the probability of separation by 4 percent.[30] Dickert-Conlin's results are largely consistent with those of Feenberg and Rosen, who estimate that for a low-income couple the marriage tax penalty combined with the EITC for two dependent children would lead to a tax refund of $359 in 1994. If those same taxpayers divorced and each filed under head-of-household status with one child, their combined tax refund would be $4,076.[31] In simple terms, the marriage tax penalty is set up such that low-income couples with dependent children have a financial incentive to divorce. As the EITC is phased out with increasing income, a married couple faces higher tax rates, whereas the cohabiting couple does not. As Dickert-Conlin states, "Although marital status, per se, does not affect the EITC, the joint income of a two-earner family may exceed the maximum allowable income for EITC eligibility, but if the couple separates, at least one spouse with sufficiently low income may become eligible."[32]

FEMALE LABOR FORCE PARTICIPATION

The tax cuts of 2001 and 2003, enacted during the George W. Bush administration, encouraged increased labor force participation by women by easing the marginal tax rates for a secondary earner. Although the 10 percent deduction on the first $30,000 of income from the second earner is not necessarily the ideal reform to address the horizontal inequities in each tax bracket caused by joint income filing by married couples, the deduction did promote a shift toward more women working. Research by economists Bar and Leukhina confirms that labor force participation by a married woman is more responsive to tax policy changes the higher her husband's income is. Bar and Leukhina find that, as a result of Reagan-era tax reforms that reduced the marriage tax penalty, there was a 30 percent increase in labor force participation by women whose husbands earned over $84,000.[33]

By examining the aggregate effect of tax reforms that reduced the marriage tax penalty on two-earner employment, Barry Bosworth and Gary Burtless find that in the 1980s married women's annual number of hours of paid work increased by 7.1 percent, most significantly among the bottom quintile of income.[34] Controlling for demographic trends of higher female salary levels (and higher levels of education), economists Nada Eissa and Hilary Hoynes find that "about 55–60 percent of the change in the marriage tax is due to changing the tax laws."[35]

However, in some cases, particularly for low-income married women, the EITC actually decreased female labor force participation (by 2 to 4 percent in the 1970s when the EITC was introduced and by 10 to 12 percent when it was expanded in the 1990s).[36] Bar and Leukhina find that, combined with the EITC, "Secondary income is heavily taxed, because it often disqualifies the [married] couple from the credit or reduces it substantially."[37]

These data indicate that the filing of joint income tax returns seems to discourage labor force participation by women across all income levels. A shift in tax policy toward marriage neutrality may increase female labor force participation among low- and high-wage earners alike.

CONCLUSION

As Alm and Whittington state,

> In particular, although the *initial* decision to cohabit versus marry is only somewhat affected by the tax consequences, the decision to make the *transition* from cohabitation to marriage is much more significantly affected by taxes. Put differently—and colloquially—the initial decision seems determined more by "passion" than "economics," but "cold reality" seems more likely to enter the calculus of the transition decision.[38]

If politicians desire to uphold the prominence of marriage, the federal government should not penalize the institution through the tax code. The alternative of cohabitation is commonly chosen in the face of significant financial penalty. Even from a labor force perspective, more equal treatment of a higher-income, two-earner family could have significant implications for macroeconomic growth as labor force participation rates rise. In 1998, the Joint Economic Committee considered three different proposals to alleviate the marriage tax penalty: (a) empowering married couples to select individual filing rather than requiring joint filing, (b) income splitting, and (c) a second-earner deduction.[39] The second-earner deduction became law as part of the Economic Growth and Tax Relief Reconciliation Act of 2001. This deduction has reduced the tax penalty for married couples and encouraged female participation in the labor force, but it represents only a Band-Aid solution to tax reform.

Income splitting is a tax reform that maintains joint filing status but adjusts for differences in tax schedules between single and joint filers.[40] The effect of such a reform would be that nearly all couples would see a reduced marriage penalty or an increased marriage bonus. Generally, under 50–50 income splitting, the joint income deduction is twice the single deduction, and the width of the joint filing bracket is calculated by doubling single-filer tax brackets. For single-earner joint filers, the marriage bonus would generally increase, whereas any existing marriage penalty would be decreased (or bonus increased) for two-earner joint filers. Income splitting could either encourage or discourage women's labor force participation rates. To the extent that income splitting would result in a lower tax rate for secondary earners in a couple, it could encourage labor force participation. Although the marginal unit of additional income may be taxed at a lower rate for secondary earners, income splitting reduces the marginal rate for the primary earner. Therefore, this reform may encourage longer hours of work for one spouse rather than entry into the labor market by the other. Although income splitting increases horizontal equality for single-earner couples and for two-earner couples with the same adjusted gross income, the reform does not treat marriage in a tax-neutral manner. A number of countries have therefore moved from taxing the family as a unit to taxing the individual earner.[41]

The income tax reform that best promotes horizontal equality and treats marriage in a tax-neutral manner would require individual filing regardless of marital status. As a 1998 Joint Economic Committee publication states, "Marriage neutrality can only be achieved by reverting to a system of individual filing or through fundamental tax reform."[42] Politically acceptable policy recommendations tend to define the unit of taxation as the individual rather than the family.[43] Both the marriage tax bonus and the marriage tax penalty would be eliminated with the use of an individual schedule of taxation for all taxpayers.[44] Eliminating the marriage tax penalty would enable couples deciding whether to marry to do so without worrying about their changing tax status. And if the marriage tax bonus were removed, national economic growth would benefit from the skills of secondary earners no longer financially discouraged from entering the labor force. As noted earlier, the United States is one of only seven countries in the Organisation for Economic Co-operation and Development to require joint income tax filing by married couples.

The Joint Economic Committee study raises concerns that giving couples the option of filing jointly or as two single individuals would increase the complexity of the US tax code. Although such a reform could increase the cost of complying with the federal income tax system, greater horizontal equality among taxpayers regardless of marital status would be promoted at the same time as encouraging greater labor force participation. However, using a mandatory single-filer system would eliminate that complexity.

The potential effects on vertical equality are worth noting, and changes to the width of tax brackets may be necessary. If policymakers want to subsidize stay-at-home parents through the tax code, the value of their noneconomic labor could be recognized by an expansion of the child tax credit and dependent deduction rather than through mandatory filing based on marital status.

The joint income filing requirement for married couples creates horizontal inequalities among couples at nearly every level of income depending on marital status. It also penalizes women for participating in the labor force. Joint income filing made more sense in the 1940s, when men tended to be higher paid than women and fewer two-earner households existed. Today, both spouses often work, and women are often the top earner in a household.

Given that a move to a single-taxpayer filing system for single and married people alike might be difficult to achieve politically, married couples should, at a minimum, be given the freedom to choose which filing status is best for them—filing a joint return as a married couple or filing separate individual tax returns as if they were unmarried taxpayers (as opposed to the current system, which penalizes married taxpayers who file separately by lowering the income thresholds at which marginal tax rates apply). Although allowing taxpayers to choose for themselves which filing status is best would still result in a marriage tax bonus for some couples, it would remove the marriage tax penalty altogether. Fostering the economic contributions of a married, educated workforce would be a major step toward creating a simpler, more equitable tax code.

CONCLUSION
Key Principles for Successful, Sustainable Tax Reform

The most basic goal of tax policy is to raise enough revenue to meet the government's spending requirements while having the least impact on market behavior.[1] But as the chapters in this book have shown, the US tax code has long failed to meet this aim: By distorting market decisions and the allocation of resources, the tax code distorts behavior, hampers job creation, and impedes both potential economic growth and potential tax revenue.

Although agreement on the need for tax reform appears to be widespread, there is no consensus—between or within political parties—on specific elements of reform. But academic research highlighted in this book suggests that a successful tax revenue system should have the following characteristics:

- *Simplicity.* The complexity of the present tax system makes compliance difficult and costly. Congress should make the tax code as simple and transparent as possible so as to increase compliance and reduce associated costs.

- *Equity.* The existing tax code is riddled with policies intended to benefit or penalize select individuals and groups. These policies result in immeasurable unintended consequences. Fairness is subjective, but any attempt to attain income tax fairness would at least reduce the number of provisions in the tax code that favor one group or economic activity over another. The federal government should not be in the business of picking winners and losers.

- *Efficiency.* Because the tax code alters market decisions in areas such as work, saving, investment, and job creation, it impedes economic growth and reduces potential tax revenue. An efficient tax system must provide sufficient revenue to fund the government's essential services but have minimal impact on taxpayer behavior.

- *Permanency and predictability.* The negative effects of the current tax code result not just from what it does today but also from what it may do in the future. Such uncertainty deters economic growth. An environment conducive to growth (and thus increased revenue as a result of a larger economy) requires a tax code that provides both near- and long-term predictability. Temporary tax provisions should be avoided. Instead, the focus should be on ways to increase economic growth, saving, and investment, keeping in mind that a larger economy will result in larger tax revenue.

There is broad consensus across academic research as to which tax policies are most likely to promote solid, sustainable economic growth and tax revenue—and which policies are most likely to fail. The following principles stand out:

- *Lower the rates of taxation.* Extensive economic research has found this most basic effect: the more you tax capital or labor, the less you get of both. The research also makes clear that incentives matter. Successful tax reform will lower both individual and corporate tax rates.

- *Avoid double taxation.* For economic efficiency, it is important that income be taxed once and only once. There is much concern that those who report significant earnings from capital gains or dividends are taxed at a lower rate than those who have only earned income. But this way of thinking fails to accurately reflect the incidence of the corporate income tax, which is increasingly borne by workers as our economy continues to rely on free trade and open markets.

- *Broaden the tax base and eliminate loopholes.* One of the key principles to successful fiscal reform is to move away from a spending system that depends on an easily manipulated income tax system. Tax reform should lower rates, broaden the tax base, and eliminate loopholes. Such changes will increase stability and lead to greater economic growth, added employment, and perhaps even increased tax revenue.

- *Reduce bad incentives.* Predictable tax policy is essential to long-term economic growth. Generally, policymakers should avoid temporary tax provisions, especially when trying to correct or rectify a permanent problem. Furthermore, allowing any provisions that favor one group or activity over another only puts the government in the position of picking winners and losers.

History has shown that tax reforms seldom last when special interests have substantial incentives to lobby Congress for tax breaks. Making the tax code as simple—by taxing a broad base at the same low rate—and as transparent as possible will help reduce the ability and incentives to reverse future tax reforms.

The current tax code is detrimental to our economy. Our tax system distorts market decisions and the allocation of resources. It hampers job creation and impedes both potential economic growth and potential tax revenue. Tax expenditures also set up a system that allows the federal government to discriminate among taxpayers by picking winners and losers. Provisions and reforms that level the playing field so that everyone plays by the same rules should be promoted over those that discriminate. Only by removing the distortions of the current tax code can the United States realize its economic potential.

Effective Tax Rates by Industry

Figure A.1. Aggregate Effective Tax Rates across All Industries

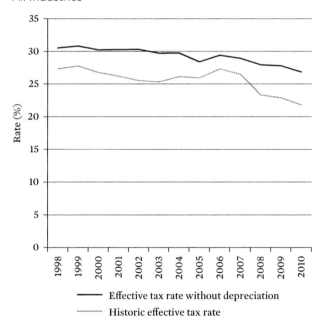

—— Effective tax rate without depreciation

·········· Historic effective tax rate

Source: Data from Internal Revenue Service, "Table 12—Returns of Active Corporations, Other than Forms 1120-REIT, 1120-RIC, and 1120S" (1998–2012), June 27, 2014.

Figure A.2. Effective Tax Rates in the Agriculture, Forestry, Fishing, and Hunting Industry

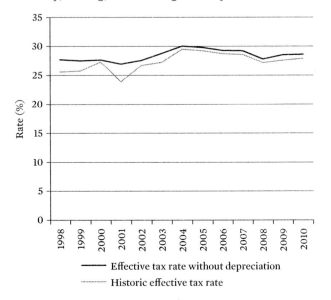

—— Effective tax rate without depreciation

·········· Historic effective tax rate

Source: Data from Internal Revenue Service, "Table 12—Returns of Active Corporations, Other than Forms 1120-REIT, 1120-RIC, and 1120S" (1998–2012), June 27, 2014.

Figure A.3. Effective Tax Rates in the Mining Industry

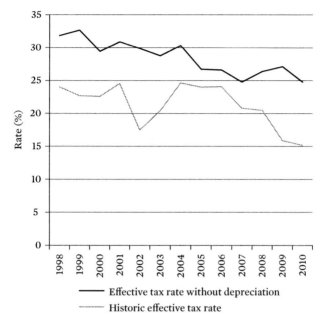

Legend:
——— Effective tax rate without depreciation
········· Historic effective tax rate

Source: Data from Internal Revenue Service, "Table 12—Returns of Active Corporations, Other than Forms 1120-REIT, 1120-RIC, and 1120S" (1998–2012), June 27, 2014.

Figure A.4. Effective Tax Rates in the Utilities Industry

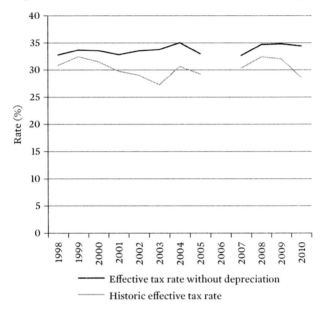

Effective tax rate without depreciation

Historic effective tax rate

Source: Data from Internal Revenue Service, "Table 12—Returns of Active Corporations, Other than Forms 1120-REIT, 1120-RIC, and 1120S" (1998–2012), June 27, 2014.

Note: Data for the utilities industry are unavailable for 2006.

Figure A.5. Effective Tax Rates in the Construction Industry

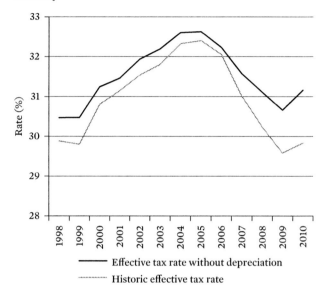

— Effective tax rate without depreciation

⋯⋯⋯ Historic effective tax rate

Source: Data from Internal Revenue Service, "Table 12—Returns of Active Corporations, Other than Forms 1120-REIT, 1120-RIC, and 1120S" (1998–2012), June 27, 2014.

Figure A.6. Effective Tax Rates in the Manufacturing Industry

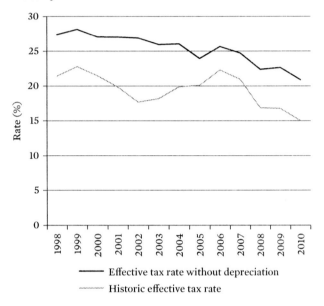

Source: Data from Internal Revenue Service, "Table 12—Returns of Active Corporations, Other than Forms 1120-REIT, 1120-RIC, and 1120S" (1998–2012), June 27, 2014.

Figure A.7. Effective Tax Rates in the Wholesale Trade Industry

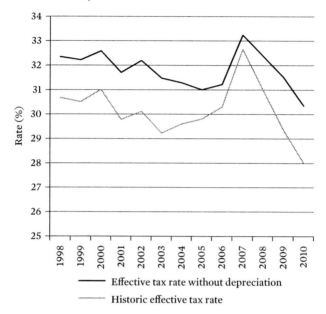

Effective tax rate without depreciation

Historic effective tax rate

Source: Data from Internal Revenue Service, "Table 12—Returns of Active Corporations, Other than Forms 1120-REIT, 1120-RIC, and 1120S" (1998–2012), June 27, 2014.

Figure A.8. Effective Tax Rates in the Retail Trade Industry

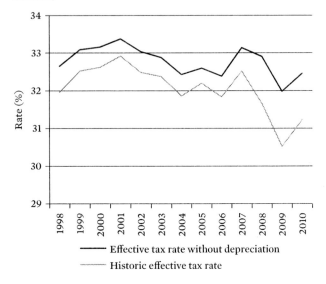

Source: Data from Internal Revenue Service, "Table 12—Returns of Active Corporations, Other than Forms 1120-REIT, 1120-RIC, and 1120S" (1998–2012), June 27, 2014.

Figure A.9. Effective Tax Rates in the Transportation and Warehousing Industry

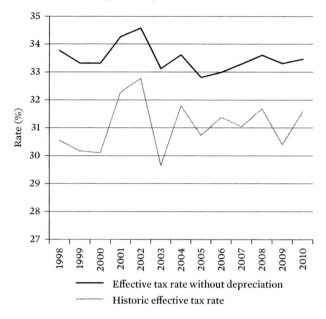

Source: Data from Internal Revenue Service, "Table 12—Returns of Active Corporations, Other than Forms 1120-REIT, 1120-RIC, and 1120S" (1998–2012), June 27, 2014.

Figure A.10. Effective Tax Rates in the Information Industry

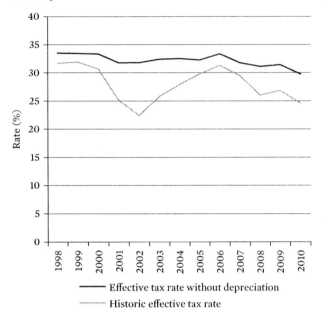

Effective tax rate without depreciation

Historic effective tax rate

Source: Data from Internal Revenue Service, "Table 12—Returns of Active Corporations, Other than Forms 1120-REIT, 1120-RIC, and 1120S" (1998–2012), June 27, 2014.

Figure A.11. Effective Tax Rates in the Finance and Insurance Industry

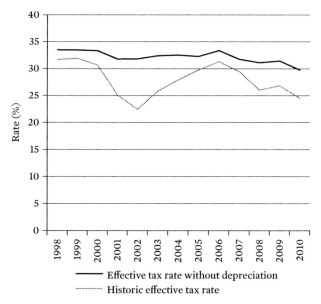

Source: Data from Internal Revenue Service, "Table 12—Returns of Active Corporations, Other than Forms 1120-REIT, 1120-RIC, and 1120S" (1998–2012), June 27, 2014.

Figure A.12. Effective Tax Rates in the Health Care and Social Assistance Industry

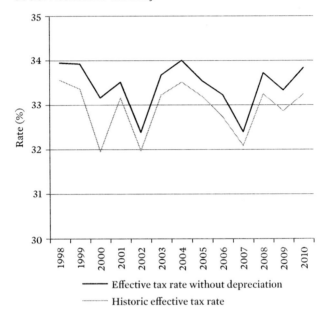

Source: Data from Internal Revenue Service, "Table 12—Returns of Active Corporations, Other than Forms 1120-REIT, 1120-RIC, and 1120S" (1998-2012), June 27, 2014.

NOTES

INTRODUCTION: WHAT ARE THE GOALS OF TAX POLICY?

1. It should be noted at the outset that meeting the government's spending requirements is not a mandate to raise taxes to higher levels to support even higher levels of government spending. Although good tax reform will increase economic growth and such growth will increase tax revenue to some extent, the United States spends more money than it collects and needs to reduce its spending. Discussions on how the federal government should reduce spending are outside the scope of this book, but interested readers looking for ideas can start here: Jason Fichtner, "The 1 Percent Solution," Mercatus Working Paper 11-05, Mercatus Center at George Mason University, Arlington, VA, February 25, 2011.

2. *Hearing on Tax Reform: Lessons from the Tax Reform Act of 1986 before the United States Committee on Finance*, 111th Cong., 2nd session (September 23, 2010) (testimony of Randall D. Weiss, managing director of economic research, The Conference Board, New York, "How Did the 1986 Tax Reform Act Attract So Much Support?").

3. Jason Fichtner and Katelyn Christ, "Uncertainty and Taxes: A Fatal Policy Mix," Mercatus Working Paper 10-74, Mercatus Center at George Mason University, Arlington, VA, December 2010.

4. Christina D. Romer and David H. Romer, "The Macroeconomic Effects of Tax Changes: Estimates Based on a New Measure of Fiscal Shocks," *American Economic Review* 100, no. 3 (June 2010): 763–801.

5. Jeffrey Miron, "The Negative Consequences of Government Expenditure," Mercatus Working Paper 10-55, Mercatus Center at George Mason University, Arlington, VA, September 2010.

6. William C. Randolph, "International Burdens of the Corporate Income Tax," Working Paper 2006-09, Congressional Budget Office, Washington, DC, August 2006.

7. Stephen J. Entin, "The Tax Treatment of Capital Assets and Its Effect on Growth: Expensing, Depreciation, and the Concept of Cost Recovery in the Tax System," Background Paper 67, Tax Foundation, Washington, DC, April 2013.

8. Edward L. Glaeser and Jesse M. Shapiro, "The Benefits of the Home Mortgage Interest Deduction," in *Tax Policy and the Economy*, ed. James M. Poterba, 37–82 (Cambridge, MA: MIT Press, 2003).

CHAPTER 1: WHAT ARE THE HIDDEN COSTS OF TAX COMPLIANCE?

1. The Joint Committee on Taxation lists 60 different federal tax provisions (excluding temporary disaster relief provisions) that were scheduled to expire in 2011. An additional 41 provisions were scheduled to expire in 2012. See Joint Committee on Taxation (JCT), "List of Expiring Federal Tax Provisions 2011–2022," JCX-1-12, Washington, DC, January 6, 2012. Some of these provisions were extended for an additional five years under the American Taxpayer Relief Act of 2012.

2. Congressional Budget Office (CBO), "The Budget and Economic Outlook: Fiscal Years 2013 to 2023," Washington, DC, February 2013, table 1-1, 9.

3. The bulk of the remaining tax revenue generated comes from social insurance and retirement taxes, which accounted for 36 percent of total revenue collected in 2011. See Office of Management and Budget, "Receipts by Source as Percentages of GDP: 1934–2017," table 2.1, http://www.whitehouse.gov /sites/default/files/omb/budget/fy2013/assets/hist02z1.xls.

4. Taxpayer Advocate Service, *National Taxpayer Advocate 2010 Annual Report to Congress*, vol. 1 (Washington, DC: IRS, 2010), 4.

5. See Seth H. Giertz and Jacob M. Feldman, "The Economic Costs of Tax Policy Uncertainty: Implications for Fundamental Tax Reform," Mercatus Research, Mercatus Center at George Mason University, Arlington, VA, November 27, 2012. See also Kevin M. Murphy, Andrei Shleifer, and Robert W. Vishny, "The Allocation of Talent: Implications for Growth," *Quarterly Journal of Economics* 106, no. 2 (1991): 503–30.

6. Authors' calculations based on IRS, "Tax Gap for Tax Year 2006," January 6, 2012.

7. US Government Accountability Office, "Tax Gap: IRS Could Significantly Increase Revenues by Better Targeting Enforcement Resources," GAO-13-151, Washington, DC, December 2012, 24.

8. Yuriy Gorodnichenko, Jorge Martinez-Vazquez, and Klara Sabirianova Peter, "Myth and Reality of Flat Tax Reform: Micro Estimates of Tax Evasion Response and Welfare Effects in Russia," *Journal of Political Economy* 117, no. 3 (2009): 504–54.

9. According to the Joint Committee on Taxation, adjusted gross income is computed by subtracting "trade or business expenses, capital losses, and contributions to a tax-qualified retirement plan by a self-employed individual, contributions to individual retirement arrangements ('IRAs'), certain moving expenses, certain education-related expenses, and alimony payments" from gross income. JCT, "Overview of the Federal Tax System as in Effect for 2012," JCX-18-12, Washington, DC, February 24, 2012, 2. See also Susan C. Nelson and Julie-Anne Cronin, "Adjusted Gross Income," in *The Encyclopedia of Taxation and Tax Policy*, ed. Joseph J. Cordes, Robert D. Ebel, and Jane G. Gravelle, 2–4 (Washington, DC: Urban Institute Press, 2005).

10. See JCT, "Overview of the Federal Tax System," 3:

> Personal exemptions generally are allowed for the taxpayer, his or her spouse, and any dependents. For 2012, the amount deductible for each personal exemption is $3,800. This amount is indexed annually for inflation. In tax years beginning after 2012, the personal exemption phaseout ('PEP') will reduce a taxpayer's personal exemption by two percent for each $2,500 by which the taxpayer's AGI [adjusted gross income] exceeds a certain threshold. JCT staff estimates of the PEP thresholds in 2013 are $172,250 (single) and $258,350 (married filing jointly).

11. Ibid.:

> The basic standard deduction varies depending upon a taxpayer's filing status. For 2012, the amount of the standard deduction is $5,950 for single individuals and married individuals filing separate returns, $8,500 for heads of households, and $11,900 for married individuals filing a joint return and surviving spouses. An additional standard deduction is allowed with respect to any individual who is elderly or blind. The amounts of the basic standard deduction and the additional standard deductions are indexed annually for inflation.

12. Ibid.:

> The deductions that may be itemized include State and
> local income taxes (or, in lieu of income, sales taxes),
> real property and certain personal property taxes, home
> mortgage interest, charitable contributions, certain invest-
> ment interest, medical expenses (in excess of 7.5 percent
> of AGI), casualty and theft losses (in excess of 10 percent
> of AGI and in excess of $100 per loss), and certain miscel-
> laneous expenses (in excess of two percent of AGI). In tax
> years beginning after 2012, the total amount of itemized
> deductions allowed is reduced for taxpayers with incomes
> over a certain threshold amount, which is indexed annually
> for inflation. JCT staff estimates of these limitation thres-
> holds in 2013 are $172,250 for both single taxpayers and
> those who are married filing jointly.

> The percentage of taxpayers who itemize deductions is cal-
> culated from data from IRS, table 1.1, "All Returns: Selected
> Income and Tax Items, by Size and Accumulated Size of
> Adjusted Gross Income, Tax Year 2010," http://www.irs
> .gov/file_source/PUP/taxstats/indtaxstats/10in11si.xls, and
> IRS, table 3, "Returns with Itemized Deductions: Itemized
> Deductions by Type and by Size of Adjusted Gross Income,
> Tax Year 2010," http://www.irs.gov/file_source/pub/irs-soi
> /10in03id.xls.

13. The alternative minimum tax exemption amount for tax year
    2013 is $51,900 ($80,800 for married couples filing jointly).
    A minimum tax rate of 26 percent applies to income earned
    above the exemption. See IRS, "Annual Inflation Adjustments
    for 2013," news release IR-2013-4, January 11, 2013.

14. C. Fritz Foley, Jay C. Hartzell, Sheridan Titman, and Garry
    Twite, "Why Do Firms Hold So Much Cash? A Tax-Based
    Explanation," Harvard Business School, Cambridge, MA,
    February 2007.

15. Active foreign-source income is subject to taxation only on
    repatriation, whereas passive foreign-source income and roy-
    alties are subject to taxation during the tax year in which they
    are generated.

16. Kate Linebaugh, "How Firms Tap Overseas Cash," *Wall Street
    Journal*, March 28, 2013.

17. John D. McKinnon, "Big Business Spars over Rewriting Tax
    Code," *Wall Street Journal*, March 28, 2013.

18. See *Hearing on Tax Reform Options: Incentives for Home-
    ownership before the United States Senate Committee on*

Finance, 112th Cong., 1st sess. (October 6, 2011) (testimony of Robert Dietz, assistant vice president for tax and policy issues, National Association of Home Builders).

19. Taxpayer Advocate Service, *National Taxpayer Advocate 2010*, vol. 1, 5.

20. Treasury Inspector General for Tax Administration, "Analysis of Internal Revenue Service Employees' Use of Tax Preparation Assistance," report 2012-40-001, Department of the Treasury, Washington, DC, January 9, 2012, 1. However, tax software may not address all taxpayer responsibilities, as former Treasury Secretary Timothy Geithner can attest. See Mary Pilon, "TurboTax and Timothy Geithner's Tax Problems," *Wallet* (blog), January 22, 2009, http://blogs.wsj.com/wallet/2009 /01/22/turbo-tax-and-timothy-geithners-tax-problems/.

21. Taxpayer Advocate Service, *National Taxpayer Advocate 2012 Annual Report to Congress*, vol. 1 (Washington, DC: IRS, 2010), 9.

22. Josh Hicks, "IRS Ombudsman: Overly Complex Tax Code Needs Overhaul," *Washington Post*, January 9, 2013.

23. Ibid.

24. Treasury Inspector General for Tax Administration, *Semiannual Report to Congress: April 1, 2011–September 30, 2011* (Washington, DC: Department of the Treasury), 30–31.

25. In this chapter, various estimates from the scholarly literature are used to assign dollar values to the "costs" of the US tax code so that readers can understand and put meaning to their impact. These figures are estimates. Moreover, a dollar in compliance costs would not necessarily have the same economic impact as, or be equivalent in magnitude to, costs associated with a dollar of defense spending, a dollar of health care spending, a dollar of government stimulus spending, and so forth.

26. Arthur B. Laffer, Wayne H. Winegarden, and John Childs, "The Economic Burden Caused by Tax Code Complexity," Laffer Center, Austin, TX, April 2011.

27. These companies are Exxon Mobil, Chevron, Apple, Microsoft, Ford Motor, JPMorgan Chase, American International Group, Wells Fargo, IBM, Wal-Mart Stores, General Electric, Intel, ConocoPhillips, Procter & Gamble, Citigroup, Berkshire Hathaway, Pfizer, Google, Johnson & Johnson, General Motors, Philip Morris International, Coca-Cola, Oracle, Hewlett-Packard, and MetLife.

28. US Census Bureau, *State and County QuickFacts* database, http://quickfacts.census.gov/qfd/. Data are for 2011.

29. CNN Money, "Top Companies: Biggest Employers," May 21, 2012.

30. Alan Auerbach and James Hines describe the effects and problem of deadweight loss as follows: "A major practical difficulty in measuring the excess burden of a single tax, or of a system of taxes, is that excess burden is a function of demand interactions that are potentially very difficult to measure. . . . In order to estimate the excess burden of a labor-income tax, it is in principle necessary to estimate the effect of the tax on . . . decision margins." See Alan J. Auerbach and James R. Hines Jr., "Taxation and Economic Efficiency," in *Handbook of Public Economics*, vol. 3, ed. Alan J. Auerbach and Martin S. Feinstein, 1347–421 (Amsterdam: Elsevier, 2002), 1359.

31. Giertz and Feldman, "Economic Costs of Tax Policy Uncertainty."

32. Arnold C. Harberger, "Taxation, Resource Allocation, and Welfare," in *The Role of Direct and Indirect Taxes in the Federal Reserve System*, ed. John Due, 25–80 (Princeton, NJ: Princeton University Press, 1964). See also Arnold C. Harberger, "The Measurement of Waste," *American Economic Review* 54 (1964): 58–76. Using labor supply as a proxy for deadweight loss, Harberger finds an increasingly negative effect on the number of individuals looking for work as marginal tax rates increase. He finds that personal income taxes reduce labor supply by a minimum of 2.5 percent among earners with the lowest marginal tax rate (20 percent) to a high of 11.38 percent for workers in the highest marginal tax rate (91 percent).

33. Martin Feldstein, "Tax Avoidance and the Deadweight Loss of the Income Tax," *Review of Economics and Statistics* 81, no. 4 (November 1999): 674–80.

34. Martin Feldstein, "Effects of Taxes on Economic Behavior," *National Tax Journal* 61, no. 1 (March 2008): 131–39.

35. Alexander Eichler, "10 Most Profitable U.S. Corporations Paid Average Tax Rate of Just 9 Percent Last Year: Report," *Huffington Post*, August 6, 2012.

36. Sören Blomquist and Laurent Simula, "Marginal Deadweight Loss When the Income Tax Is Nonlinear," Uppsala University and Uppsala Center for Fiscal Studies, Uppsala, Sweden, March 8, 2012.

37. These numbers are the authors' calculations. See CBO, "Historical Budget Data—February 2013 Baseline Projections," February 2013, table 1, http://www.cbo.gov/sites/default/files /cbofiles/attachments/43904-Historical%20Budget%20Data

-2.xls, and CBO, "Budget and Economic Outlook: Fiscal Years 2013 to 2023," summary table 1, 3.

38. Seth Giertz, "The Elasticity of Taxable Income: Influences on Economic Efficiency and Tax Revenues, and Implications for Tax Policy," in *Tax Policy Lessons from the 2000s*, ed. Alan D. Viard, 101–36 (Washington, DC: AEI Press, 2009).

39. Percentages are the authors' calculations.

40. Raj Chetty, "Is the Taxable Income Elasticity Sufficient to Calculate Deadweight Loss? The Implications of Evasion and Avoidance," *American Economic Journal: Economic Policy* 1, no. 2 (August 2009): 31–52.

41. Joel Slemrod and Shlomo Yitzhaki, "Tax Avoidance, Evasion, and Administration," in *Handbook of Public Economics*, vol. 3, ed. Alan J. Auerbach and Martin S. Feinstein, 1423–70 (Amsterdam: Elsevier, 2002).

42. Chetty, "Is the Taxable Income Elasticity Sufficient to Calculate Deadweight Loss?"

43. Brian Kelleher Richter, Krislert Samphantharak, and Jeffrey F. Timmons, "Lobbying and Taxes," *American Journal of Political Science* 53, no. 4 (October 2009): 893–909.

44. Hui Chen, David Parsley, and Ya-Wen Yang, "Corporate Lobbying and Financial Performance," Working Paper, University of Colorado–Boulder, Boulder, November 23, 2012.

45. Murphy, Shleifer, and Vishny, "Allocation of Talent."

46. Giertz and Feldman, "Economic Costs of Tax Policy Uncertainty."

47. Federico Sturzenegger and Mariano Tommasi, "The Distribution of Political Power, the Costs of Rent-Seeking, and Economic Growth," *Economic Inquiry* 32, no. 2 (April 1994): 236–48, 237.

48. Anil Kumar, "Labor Supply, Deadweight Loss, and Tax Reform Act of 1986: A Nonparametric Evaluation Using Panel Data," *Journal of Public Economics* 92 (2008): 236–53, 238.

49. Gorodnichenko, Martinez-Vazquez, and Peter, "Myth and Reality of Flat Tax Reform."

50. IRS, "Tax Gap for Tax Year 2006."

51. The $385 billion figure is from IRS, "Tax Gap for Tax Year 2006." Other numbers are the authors' calculations. See CBO, "Budget and Economic Outlook: Fiscal Years 2013 to 2023," table B-1.

52. See Jane G. Gravelle, "Tax Havens: International Tax Avoidance and Evasion," Report 7-5700, Congressional Research Service, Washington, DC, January 23, 2013. Gravelle's

range of estimates (corporate: $10 billion to $60 billion; individual: $40 billion to $70 billion) come from the following studies: Martin Sullivan, "Shifting Profits Offshore Costs US Treasury $10 Billion or More," *Tax Notes*, September 27, 2004, 1477–81; Kimberly A. Clausing, "The Revenue Effects of Multinational Firm Income Shifting," *Tax Notes*, March 28, 2011, 1580–86; Joseph Guttentag and Reven Avi-Yonah, "Closing the International Tax Gap," in *Bridging the Tax Gap: Addressing the Crisis in Federal Tax Administration*, ed. Max B. Sawicky, 99–110 (Washington, DC: Economic Policy Institute, 2005).

53. Joel Slemrod, "Cheating Ourselves: The Economics of Tax Evasion," *Journal of Economic Perspectives* 21, no. 1 (2007): 25–48.

54. Jason J. Fichtner and Jacob Feldman, "The Hidden Costs of Tax Compliance," Mercatus Research, Mercatus Center at George Mason University, Arlington, VA, May 2013.

55. Ibid.

CHAPTER 2: WHAT CAN BE LEARNED FROM THE TAX REFORM ACT OF 1986?

1. *Hearing on Tax Reform: Lessons from the Tax Reform Act of 1986 before the United States Senate Committee on Finance*, 111th Cong., 2nd session (September 23, 2010) (testimony of Randall D. Weiss, managing director of economic research, The Conference Board, New York, "How Did the 1986 Tax Reform Act Attract So Much Support?"). Note: Many of these provisions were renewed with the Tax Relief, Unemployment Insurance Reauthorization, and Job Creation Act of 2010.

2. The Joint Committee on Taxation's estimation of the revenue effects of the Tax Increase Prevention Act of 2014 are available at https://www.jct.gov/publications.html?func=startdown &id=4677.

3. For a discussion of what is and is not a tax expenditure, see Donald B. Marron, "Spending in Disguise," *National Affairs* 8 (Summer 2011): 20–34.

4. Ibid, 25–26.

5. Ibid, 26.

6. Edward D. Kleinbard, "The Congress within the Congress: How Tax Expenditures Distort Our Budget and Our Political Processes," *Ohio Northern University Law Review* 36 (2010): 1–30, 15.

7. Edward A. Zelinsky, "James Madison and Public Choice at Gucci Gulch: A Procedural Defense of Tax Expenditures and

Tax Institutions," *Yale Law Journal* 102, no. 5 (March 1993): 1165–207, 1176–77.

8. Ibid., 1182–83.

9. Paul McDaniel, "Tax Expenditures as Tools of Government Action," in *Beyond Privatization: The Tools of Government Action*, ed. Lester M. Salamon (Washington, DC: Urban Institute Press, 1989), 178.

10. Kleinbard, "Congress within the Congress," 18.

11. Ibid.

12. Edward D. Kleinbard, "Tax Expenditure Framework Legislation," Law Economics Working Paper 109, University of Southern California Law School, Los Angeles, 2010, 4.

13. Kleinbard, "Congress within the Congress," 21.

14. Authors' calculations; Jane G. Gravelle and Laurence J. Kotlikoff, "Corporate Taxation and the Efficiency Gains of the 1986 Tax Reform Act," *Economic Theory* 6, no. 1 (February 1995): 51–81, 52.

15. Don Fullerton and Yolanda Henderson, "The Impact of Fundamental Tax Reform on the Allocation of Resources," NBER Working Paper 1904, National Bureau of Economic Research, Cambridge, MA, April 1986.

16. Ibid., 16.

17. The implicit federal subsidization of home mortgage interest rates through Fannie Mae and Freddie Mac also contributed to overinvestment in housing.

18. Douglas Holtz-Eakin, "The Tax Reform Act of 1986: Simplicity, Equity, and Efficiency," *Akron Tax Journal* 4 (1987): 69–82, 80–81.

19. *Hearing on Tax Reform: Lessons from the Tax Reform Act of 1986 before the United States Senate Committee on Finance*, 111th Cong., 2nd session (September 23, 2010) (testimony of John E. Chapoton, strategic advisor, Brown Advisory, Washington, DC).

20. Kleinbard, "Congress within the Congress," 14.

21. One proposed reform that addresses efficiency is Martin Feldstein's 2 percent tax expenditure ceiling, which is considered later in this chapter.

22. For a discussion of the treatment of imputed income in tax policy, see Jason J. Fichtner, "A Comparison of Tax Distribution Tables: How Missing or Incomplete Information Distorts Perspectives," in *The Secret Chamber or the Public Square: What Can Be Done to Make Tax Analysis and Revenue Estimation More Transparent and Accurate?* ed. Dan R.

Mastromarco, David R. Burton, and William R. Beach, 257–86 (Washington, DC: Heritage Foundation, 2005).

23. Wenli Li and Pierre-Daniel Sarte, "Progressive Taxation and Long-Run Growth," *American Economic Review* 94, no. 5 (December 2004): 1705–16.

24. Alan J. Auerbach and Joel Slemrod, "The Economic Effects of the Tax Reform Act of 1986," *Journal of Economic Literature* 35, no. 2 (June 1998): 589–632, 593–94.

25. Katherine Baicker, "Making Health Care More Affordable through Health Insurance Finance Reform," *BusinessEconomics* 42, no. 3 (July 2007): 36–37.

26. Joseph Bankman, "Reforming the Tax Preference for Employer Health Insurance," presented at the New York University School of Law Colloquium on Tax Policy and Public Finance, New York, January 20, 2011, 4.

27. Samuel Y. Sessions and Philip R. Lee, "Using Tax Reform to Drive Health Care Reform: Putting the Horse before the Cart," *Journal of the American Medical Association* 300, no. 16 (October 2008): 1929–31.

28. Holtz-Eakin, "Tax Reform Act of 1986," 77.

29. Joint Committee on Taxation, "Estimates of Federal Tax Expenditures for Fiscal Years 2012–2017," Document 78-317, Washington, DC, February 1, 2013.

30. Eric. J. Toder, Benjamin H. Harris, and Katherine Lim, "Distributional Effects of Tax Expenditures," Tax Policy Center, Urban Institute–Brookings Institution, Washington, DC, July 2009, 1–2.

31. Auerbach and Slemrod, "Economic Effects of the Tax Reform Act of 1986," 593.

32. Matthew Mitchell and Andrea Castillo, "What Went Wrong with the Bush Tax Cuts," Mercatus Research Paper, Mercatus Center at George Mason University, Arlington, VA, November 28, 2012.

33. *Hearing on Tax Reform: Lessons from the Tax Reform Act of 1986* (testimony of Chapoton), 9.

34. Leonard E. Burman, Christopher Geissler, and Eric J. Toder, "How Big Are Total Individual Income Tax Expenditures, and Who Benefits from Them?" *American Economic Review* 98, no. 2 (May 2008): 79–83, 82.

35. Ibid.

36. Ibid., 83.

37. Holtz-Eakin, "Tax Reform Act of 1986," 75.

38. Joel Slemrod, "Did the Tax Reform Act of 1986 Simplify Tax Matters?," *Journal of Economic Perspectives* 6, no. 1 (Winter 1992): 47–57, 51.

39. Ibid., 50.

40. Marsha Blumenthal and Joel Slemrod, "The Compliance Cost of the U.S. Individual Income Tax System: A Second Look after Tax Reform," *National Tax Journal* 45, no. 2 (June 1992): 185–202, 186.

41. Holtz-Eakin, "Tax Reform Act of 1986," 74.

42. Slemrod, "Did the Tax Reform Act of 1986 Simplify Tax Matters?," 55–56.

43. The Joint Committee on Taxation states: "It should be noted that counting the number of tax expenditures involves a certain amount of arbitrariness, since the number of tax expenditures reported in any particular year is sensitive to the level of disaggregation any piece of legislation or set of provisions is judged to warrant." See Joint Committee on Taxation, *Background Information on Tax Expenditure Analysis and Historical Survey of Tax Expenditure Estimates*, JCX-15-11, March 9, 2011.

44. Thomas L. Hungerford, "Tax Expenditures and the Federal Budget," Report RL34622, Congressional Research Service, Washington, DC, September 10, 2008.

45. Ibid.

46. *Hearing on Tax Reform: Lessons from the Tax Reform Act of 1986 before the United States Senate Committee on Finance*, 111th Cong., 2nd session (September 23, 2010) (testimony of Bill Archer, senior policy advisor, PricewaterhouseCoopers).

47. Joint Committee on Taxation, *Estimates of Federal Tax Expenditures for Fiscal Years 2012–2017*.

48. Office of Management and Budget, "Receipts by Source as Percentages of GDP: 1934–2017," table 2.1, http://www.whitehouse.gov/sites/default/files/omb/budget/fy2015/assets/hist02z1.xls.

49. The top 10 individual tax expenditures are estimated at $3,117.3 billion, and the top 10 corporate tax expenditures are estimated at $351.5 billion, for the five-year period between 2009 and 2014. Joint Committee on Taxation, *Background Information on Tax Expenditure Analysis*.

50. Burman, Geissler, and Toder, "How Big Are Total Individual Income Tax Expenditures?," 81–83.

51. *Hearing on Tax Reform: Lessons from the Tax Reform Act of 1986* (testimony of Chapoton).

52. Not all lobbying is considered rent-seeking behavior per se; the dissemination of educational information is an example. For this chapter, lobbying is classified as rent-seeking behavior if the purpose is mainly to gain or preserve tax preferences or government spending.

53. Randall G. Holcombe, "Tax Policy from a Public Choice Perspective," *National Tax Journal* 51, no. 2 (June 1998), 359–71, 360.

54. James M. Poterba, "Public Finance and Public Choice," *National Tax Journal* 51, no. 2 (June 1998), 391–96, 394.

55. Holcombe, "Tax Policy from a Public Choice Perspective," 364.

56. Slemrod, "Did the Tax Reform Act of 1986 Simplify Tax Matters?," 46.

57. *Hearing on Tax Reform: Lessons from the Tax Reform Act of 1986* (testimony of Weiss).

58. Martin Feldstein, Daniel Feenberg, and Maya MacGuineas, "Capping Individual Tax Expenditure Benefits," NBER Working Paper 16921, National Bureau of Economic Research, Cambridge, MA, April 2011, 3.

59. Ibid., 5, table 1.

60. Burman, Geissler, and Toder, "How Big are Total Individual Income Tax Expenditures?," 83.

61. Kleinbard, "Tax Expenditure Framework Legislation," 41.

62. Ibid., 42.

63. Holtz-Eakin, "Tax Reform Act of 1986," 73.

64. Gerald Prante, "Tax Reform: What Has Changed Since 1986?," Tax Policy Blog, Tax Foundation, October 10, 2006, http://www.taxfoundation.org/commentary/show/1908.html.

65. Michael J. Graetz, "Tax Reform Unraveling," *Journal of Economic Perspectives* 21, no. 1 (Winter 2007): 69–90, 87. See also Jason J. Fichtner, *Reforming the U.S. Corporate Tax System to Increase Corporate Tax Competitiveness*, report prepared for the Joint Economic Committee, 109th Cong., 1st sess., May 2005.

66. *Hearing on Tax Reform: Lessons from the Tax Reform Act of 1986* (testimony of Weiss), 5.

67. Graetz, "Tax Reform Unraveling," 71.

68. Charles E. McLure Jr. and George R. Zodrow, "Treasury I and the Tax Reform Act of 1986: The Economics and Politics of Tax Reform," *Journal of Economic Perspectives* 1, no. 1 (Summer 1987): 35–58, 57.

CHAPTER 3: WHY SHOULD CONGRESS RESTRUCTURE THE CORPORATE INCOME TAX?

1. Barack Obama, "Remarks by the President in State of Union Address," Washington, DC, January 25, 2011.

2. Scott Horsley, "Obama, Ryan Agree: Business Tax Codes Need Reform," *National Public Radio*, April 16, 2011.

3. Conor Sullivan and Cleve Jones, "Global Tax Map," *Financial Times*, April 26, 2013.

4. OECD, "Taxation of Corporate and Capital Income," table II.I, Paris, May 2013; Kevin A. Hassett and Aparna Mathur, "Report Card on Effective Corporate Tax Rates," American Enterprise Institute, Washington, DC, February 9, 2011.

5. Curtis S. Dubay, "Corporate Tax Reform Should Focus on Rate Reduction," WebMemo 3146, Heritage Foundation, Washington, DC, February 11, 2011, http://www.heritage.org /Research/Reports/2011/02/Corporate-Tax-Reform-Should -Focus-on-Rate-Reduction.

6. Jason J. Fichtner, *Reforming the U.S. Corporate Tax System to Increase Corporate Tax Competitiveness*, report prepared for the Joint Economic Committee, 109th Cong., 1st sess., May 2005.

7. The countries were Chile, Ireland, Israel, the Republic of Korea, Mexico, and the United States. See PricewaterhouseCoopers, "Evolution of Territorial Tax Systems in the OECD," prepared for the Technology CEO Council, April 2, 2013.

8. Office of Tax Policy, "Corporate Inversion Transactions: Tax Policy Implications," US Department of the Treasury, Washington, DC, May 2002.

9. *Foreign-source income* refers to income earned outside a corporation's home country. *Active income* is a category of income introduced with the Tax Reform Act of 1986. It generally refers to salaries, wages, commissions, and income from sources in which a company actively and materially participates. *Passive income* refers to revenue derived from sources such as rental real estate and income from other sources in which a company does not actively or materially participate. The distinction is important for tax purposes because passive losses are generally not allowed to be offset against active income.

10. PricewaterhouseCoopers, "Global Effective Tax Rates," prepared for Business Roundtable, April 14, 2011.

11. Hiroko Tabuchi, "Japan Will Cut Corporate Income Tax Rate," *New York Times*, December 13, 2010.

12. Scott Hode, "Countdown to #1: 2011 Marks 20th Year That U.S. Corporate Tax Rate Is Higher than OECD Average," Fiscal

Fact 261, Tax Foundation, Washington, DC, March 9, 2011. See also KPMG, "Corporate Tax Rates Table," http://www.kpmg .com/global/en/services/tax/tax-tools-and-resources/pages /corporate-tax-rates-table.aspx.

13. Canada Revenue Agency, "Corporation Tax Rates," May 6, 2015, http://www.cra-arc.gc.ca/tx/bsnss/tpcs/crprtns/rts-eng .html. Provincial rates vary from province to province.

14. Duanjie Chen and Jack Mintz, "Federal–Provincial Business Tax Reforms: A Growth Agenda with Competitive Rates and a Neutral Treatment of Business Activities," SPP Research Paper 4-1, School of Public Policy, University of Calgary, Calgary, AB, January 2011.

15. Paul Vieira, "Corporate Tax Cuts to Create 100,000 Jobs: Study," *National Post*, January 25, 2011.

16. Dubay, "Corporate Tax Reform Should Focus on Rate Reduction."

17. Business Roundtable, "Taxing American Corporations in the Global Marketplace," April 2011.

18. Seth H. Giertz and Jacob M. Feldman, "The Economic Costs of Tax Policy Uncertainty: Implications for Fundamental Tax Reform," Mercatus Research Paper, Mercatus Center at George Mason University, Arlington, VA, November 27, 2012.

19. David J. Lynch, "Does Tax Code Send U.S. Jobs Offshore?," *USA Today*, March 22, 2008.

20. David Wessel, "Big U.S. Firms Shift Hiring Abroad," *Wall Street Journal*, April 19, 2011.

21. Steven G. Horwitz, "Corporations Are Indeed People," *Austin Statesman,* August 13, 2011.

22. Fichtner, *Reforming the U.S. Corporate Tax System to Increase Competitiveness.*

23. William C. Randolph, "International Burdens of the Corporate Income Tax," Working Paper 2006-09, Congressional Budget Office, Washington, DC, August 2006.

24. Kevin A. Hassett and Aparna Mathur, "Taxes and Wages," Working Paper 128, American Enterprise Institute, Washington, DC, June 2006.

25. Simeon Djankov, Tim Ganser, Caralee McLiesh, Rita Ramalho, and Andrei Shleifer, "The Effect of Corporate Taxes on Investment and Entrepreneurship," NBER Working Paper 13756, National Bureau of Economic Research, Cambridge, MA, January 2008.

26. Richard Rubin, "U.S. Companies Are Stashing $2.1 Trillion Overseas to Avoid Taxes," *Bloomberg Business*, March 4, 2015.

See also Joint Committee on Taxation, "Estimates of Federal Tax Expenditures for Fiscal Years 2012–2017," JCS-1-13, Washington, DC, February 1, 2013, table 1.

27. OECD, "Revenue Statistics: Comparative Tables," OECD StatExtracts database, http://stats.oecd.org/Index.aspx ?DataSetCode=REV.

28. Alex Brill and Kevin Hassett, "Revenue-Maximizing Corporate Income Taxes," Working Paper 137, American Enterprise Institute, Washington, DC, July 31, 2007.

CHAPTER 4: WHY DO WORKERS BEAR A SIGNIFICANT SHARE OF THE CORPORATE INCOME TAX?

1. Benjamin Harris, senior research associate at the Brookings Institution, states:

> Determining who bears the burden of the corporate income tax is a complicated exercise. The corporate tax can influence the investment decisions of capital owners, how companies finance investment, and the international allocation of capital, and these effects can vary not only across countries but also across sectors. Changes in firm and investor decisions can then affect wages, output prices, and levels of investment, which in turn can influence the terms of trade. In sum, the complex set of economic interactions makes it difficult to isolate the impact of the corporate tax on the return to capital and land, wage rates, and consumer prices.

See Benjamin H. Harris, "Corporate Tax Incidence and Its Implications for Progressivity," Tax Policy Center, Urban Institute–Brookings Institution, Washington, DC, November 2009.

2. Jason J. Fichtner and Nick Tuszynski, "Why the United States Needs to Restructure the Corporate Income Tax," Mercatus Working Paper 11-42, Mercatus Center at George Mason University, Arlington, VA, November 2, 2011.

3. In recent changes to the understanding of who ultimately bears the costs of taxation, the Joint Committee on Taxation assumes that 75 percent of the tax is paid by owners of capital and 25 percent by workers. Joint Committee on Taxation, "Modeling the Distribution of Taxes on Business Income," JCX-14-13, Washington, DC, October 16, 2013. Slightly older methodology from the Treasury Department assumes that 82 percent of the corporate income tax is borne by capital

and 18 percent by labor. See Julie Anne Cronin, Emily Y. Lin, Laura Power, and Michael Cooper, "Distributing the Corporate Income Tax: Revised U.S. Treasury Methodology," US Treasury Department, Washington, DC, May 17, 2012. Alternatively, other studies find that labor bears a significant portion of the corporate income tax, including a paper by economists Mihir Desai, C. Fritz Foley, and James Hines, where labor bears 75 percent of the cost of capital. See Mihir A. Desai, C. Fritz Foley, and James R. Hines Jr., "Labor and Capital Shares of the Corporate Tax Burden: International Evidence," prepared for the International Tax Forum and Urban Institute–Brookings Institution Tax Policy Center Conference on Who Pays the Corporate Tax in an Open Economy, December 18, 2007. Note: The short- versus long-run effects of who bears the burden of a tax are an important consideration when evaluating the incidence of a tax. In the short run the corporate income tax may fall on either owners of capital, workers, or consumers through higher prices. In the long run, capital may relocate across industries and countries. This chapter follows the convention outlined in Joint Committee on Taxation, "Modeling the Distribution of Taxes on Business Income," which states: "Following the standard view expressed in the economic literature, the Joint Committee staff's distributional methodology assumes that none of the burden of corporate income taxes flows through to consumers. These long-run incidence assumptions match those currently made by the CBO."

4. Jennifer Gravelle, "Corporate Tax Incidence: Review of General Equilibrium Estimates and Analysis," *National Tax Journal* 66, no. 1 (March 2013): 185–214.

5. Jane G. Gravelle and Kent A. Smetters, "Does the Open Economy Assumption Really Mean That Labor Bears the Burden of a Capital Income Tax?," *Advances in Economic Analysis and Policy* 6, no. 1, article 3 (August 2006): 1–44. See also William C. Randolph, "International Burdens of the Corporate Income Tax," Working Paper 2006-09, Congressional Budget Office, Washington, DC, August 2006; R. Alison Felix, "Passing the Burden: Corporate Tax Incidence in Open Economies," Regional Research Working Paper 07-01, Federal Reserve Bank of Kansas City, Kansas City, MO, October 2007.

6. Gravelle, "Corporate Tax Incidence."

7. Marian Krzyaniak and Richard A. Musgrave, *The Shifting of the Corporation Income Tax* (Baltimore: Johns Hopkins Press, 1963).

8. Alan J. Auerbach, "Who Bears the Corporate Tax? A Review of What We Know," NBER Working Paper 11686, National Bureau of Economic Research, Washington, DC, October 2005.

9. Ergete Ferede and Bev Dahlby, "The Impact of Tax Cuts on Economic Growth: Evidence from the Canadian Provinces," *National Tax Journal* 65, no. 3 (September 2012): 563–94, 564, citing OECD, "Tax Policy Reform and Economic Growth," OECD Tax Policy Study 20, Organisation for Economic Co-operation and Development, Paris, 2010.

10. US Department of the Treasury, "General Explanations of the Administration's Fiscal Year 2015 Revenue Proposals," Washington, DC, March 2014.

11. Hans Ulrich Bacher and Marius Brülhart, "Progressive Taxes and Firm Births," *International Tax and Public Finance* 20, no. 1 (February 2013): 129–68.

12. Simeon Djankov, Tim Ganser, Caralee McLiesh, Rita Ramalho, and Andrei Shleifer, "The Effect of Corporate Taxes on Investment and Entrepreneurship," *American Economics Journal: Macroeconomics* 2, no. 3 (July 2010): 31–64.

13. Gravelle and Smetters, "Does the Open Economy Assumption Really Mean That Labor Bears the Burden of a Capital Income Tax?"

14. Randolph, "International Burdens of the Corporate Income Tax."

15. Gravelle and Smetters, "Does the Open Economy Assumption Really Mean That Labor Bears the Burden of a Capital Income Tax?"; Gravelle, "Corporate Tax Incidence"; Randolph, "International Burdens of the Corporate Income Tax."

16. James R. Melvin, "The Corporate Income Tax in an Open Economy," *Journal of Public Economics* 17, no. 3 (1982): 393–403.

17. Gravelle, "Corporate Tax Incidence."

18. Randolph, "International Burdens of the Corporate Income Tax."

19. Gravelle, "Corporate Tax Incidence."

20. Arnold C. Harberger, "The ABCs of Corporation Tax Incidence: Insights into the Open-Economy Case," in *Tax Policy and Economic Growth*, 51–73 (Washington, DC: American Council for Capital Formation Center for Policy Research, 1995).

21. John Mutti and Harry Grubert, "Empirical Asymmetries in Foreign Direct Investment and Taxation," *Journal of International Economics* 62, no. 2 (March 2004): 337–58.

22. Michael P. Devereux and Rachel Griffith, "Taxes and the Location of Production: Evidence from a Panel of US Multinationals," *Journal of Public Economics* 68, no. 3 (June 1998): 335–67. See also Sven Stöwhase, "Profit Shifting

Opportunities, Multinationals, and the Determinants of FDI," Discussion Paper in Economics 29, Ludwig Maximilian University of Munich, Munich, Germany, 2002.

23. Djankov, Ganser, McLiesh, Ramalho, and Shleifer, "Effect of Corporate Taxes," 33.

24. Harry Grubert and John Mutti, "Taxes, Tariffs, and Transfer Pricing in Multinational Corporate Decision Making," *Review of Economics and Statistics* 73, no. 2 (May 1991): 285–93. See also James R. Hines and Eric M. Rice, "Fiscal Paradise: Foreign Tax Havens and American Business," *Quarterly Journal of Economics* 109, no. 1 (February 1994): 149–82.

25. Melvin, "Corporate Income Tax in an Open Economy"; Randolph, "International Burdens of the Corporate Income Tax."

26. Desai, Foley, and Hines, "Labor and Capital Shares of the Corporate Tax Burden," 4.

27. Laurence J. Kotlikoff and Jianjun Miao, "What Does the Corporate Income Tax Tax? A Simple Model without Capital," *Annals of Economics and Finance* 14, no. 1 (May 2013): 1–19.

CHAPTER 5: HOW DOES THE CORPORATE TAX CODE DISTORT CAPITAL INVESTMENTS?

1. Stephen J. Entin, "The Tax Treatment of Capital Assets and Its Effect on Growth: Expensing, Depreciation, and the Concept of Cost Recovery in the Tax System," Background Paper 67, Tax Foundation, Washington, DC, April 2013.

2. Congressional Budget Office (CBO), "Taxing Capital Income: Effective Rates and Approaches to Reform," Washington, DC, October 2005.

3. Michael Schuyler, "Comparing the Growth and Revenue Effects of Four Proposed Depreciation Systems: Baucus, Camp, Wyden, and Full Expensing," Fiscal Fact 433, Tax Foundation, Washington, DC, June 2014.

4. For accounting purposes, assets are often depreciated using the simple straight-line method. But there are other acceptable practices, as outlined in the Financial Accounting Standards Board's Accounting Standards Codification of Generally Accepted Accounting Principles (GAAP). See also Entin, "Tax Treatment of Capital Assets"; *Hearing on Tax Reform Options: Incentives for Capital Investment and Manufacturing before the United States Senate Committee on Finance*, 112th Cong., 2nd sess. (March 6, 2012) (testimony

of Michelle Hanlon, associate professor of accounting, Massachusetts Institute of Technology).

5. The accounting process for shareholders to show profit and loss is called *book accounting,* which is different from accounting for tax purposes. Note that the effective tax rate for book purposes, as it appears to corporate executives and shareholders, does not always capture the effects of timing in the true economic sense. See *Hearing on Tax Reform Options: Incentives for Capital Investment and Manufacturing* (testimony of Hanlon).

6. The term *depreciation* often suggests that defined tax write-offs over time have some necessary link to the useful life of an asset. The term *cost recovery* is often more precise, because it refers unambiguously to recouping the original expenditure. This chapter favors the term *depreciation* over *cost recovery* for simplicity; depreciation should be understood as a cost-recovery mechanism.

7. An asset's useful life is difficult to assess because it varies by industry and by business. A piece of equipment could last 10 years if used during normal business hours but only four years if used 24 hours a day. The early evolution of asset lives illustrates this difficulty nicely. In a 1920 publication, *Bulletin F: Depreciation and Obsolescence,* the Bureau of Internal Revenue states, "It is considered impracticable to prescribe fixed, defined rates of depreciation which would be allowable for all property of a given asset or character." David W. Brazell, Lowell Dworin, and Michael Walsh, "A History of Federal Tax Depreciation Policy" (Paper 64, Office of Tax Analysis, Washington, DC, May 1989), 6.

8. IRS, "How to Depreciate Property," Publication 946, Washington, DC, February 2013, appendix B.

9. Declining-balance depreciation is often called *200 percent depreciation* because it allows double the straight-line equivalent. Depreciation is accelerated when the declining balance becomes more than 100 percent of the straight-line equivalent. See Joint Committee on Taxation (JCT), "Background and Present Law Relating to Cost Recovery and Domestic Production Activities," Washington, DC, March 6, 2012, 20–21.

10. Depreciation can be accelerated by any number of methods. Bonus depreciation and declining-balance depreciation both change the timing of a write-off within a given useful-life time frame. Depreciation can also be accelerated by shortening the time frame or useful life, often arbitrarily.

11. In 1920, the Bureau of Internal Revenue first published *Bulletin F: Depreciation and Obsolescence*, which did not list specific asset lives or depreciation schedules. The bureau asked taxpayers to estimate depreciation time lines in accordance with their own experiences. *Bulletin F* evolved through subsequent revisions, which listed industry average asset lives determined by surveys of industry depreciation. The 1942 version of *Bulletin F* became the de facto standard for asset lives and remained the standard that auditors used until 1954. See Brazell, Dworin, and Walsh, "History of Federal Tax Depreciation Policy," 6–12.

12. Ibid., 14. The *Depreciation Guidelines and Rules* were adopted in place of *Bulletin F* in July 1962.

13. Ibid., 18. These new standards were called *asset depreciation ranges* and were adapted from *Bulletin F* and modified by using research from the newly established Office of Industrial Economics.

14. Ibid., 20. This new system of tax treatment was called the *accelerated cost-recovery system*.

15. MACRS and ADS were a combination of explicit class lives dictated by Congress and a framework created by the secretary of the treasury. The secretary was able to modify the class lives until 1988. See JCT, "Background and Present Law," 21.

16. Ibid., 22. MACRS uses both 150 percent and 200 percent declining-balance accelerated depreciation.

17. Ibid., 24. ADS is required for foreign property holdings and some tax-exempt property. It is available to any taxpayer in any class of property. When given the option (which is the case for almost all types of property), businesses tend to use MACRS because it offers accelerated depreciation. Also, a list of asset classes and depreciation schedules can be found in IRS, "How to Depreciate Property," appendix A.

18. Brazell, Dworin, and Walsh, "History of Federal Tax Depreciation Policy," 12.

19. The Job Creation and Worker Assistance Act of 2002 was the first instance of bonus depreciation. During the passage of the Jobs and Growth Tax Relief Reconciliation Act of 2003, Congress explained the rationale for bonus depreciation as "to spur an economic recovery." See JCT, "Background and Present Law," 25.

20. See Job Creation and Worker Assistance Act of 2002, Pub. L. 107-147, 116 Stat. 21 (2002); Jobs and Growth Tax Relief Reconciliation Act of 2003, Pub. L. 108-27, 117 Stat. 752 (2003); American Jobs Creation Act of 2004, Pub. L.

108-357, 118 Stat. 1418 (2004); Economic Stimulus Act of 2008, Pub. L. 110-185, 122 Stat. 613 (2008); American Recovery and Reinvestment Act of 2009, Pub. L. 111-5, 123 Stat. 115 (2009); Tax Relief, Unemployment Insurance Reauthorization, and Job Creation Act of 2010, Pub. L. 111-312, 124 Stat. 3296 (2010); American Taxpayer Relief Act of 2012, Pub. L. 112-240, 126 Stat. 2313 (2013). These laws all offer some level of bonus depreciation on specific types of assets. Each law's stipulations are multifaceted, applying to several different types of property for different lengths of time, both retroactively and into the future. For a comprehensive summary of each law, see JCT, "Background and Present Law," 25–26. For the 2012 law, see Ernst & Young, "Fiscal Cliff Legislation Extends 50% Bonus Depreciation and Leasing Provisions," in *Ernst & Young Tax Guide 2013: Tax Updates* (New York: Wiley).

21. There is some debate among economists regarding the definition of *tax expenditures*. For more, see Jason J. Fichtner and Jacob Feldman, "When Are Tax Expenditures Really Spending?," Mercatus Working Paper 11-45, Mercatus Center at George Mason University, Arlington, VA, November 2011.

22. Government Accountability Office, "Corporate Tax Expenditures: Information on Estimating Revenue Losses and Related Federal Spending Programs," Washington, DC, March 2013, 11.

23. Jane G. Gravelle, "Reducing Depreciation Allowances to Finance a Lower Corporate Tax Rate," *National Tax Journal* 64, no. 4 (December 2011): 1039–54. See also CBO, *Reducing the Deficit: Spending and Revenue Options* (Washington, DC, March 2011), 180–81; JCT, "Background and Present Law," 25.

24. Gravelle, "Reducing Depreciation Allowances."

25. The time horizon is important because of the nature of accelerated and straight-line depreciation. Accelerated depreciation allows larger deductions early in the asset's life compared to the straight-line method. Hence, projected savings would be larger in the 5- or 10-year budget window, when accelerated depreciation would have allowed larger deductions. At the end of an asset's life, straight-line depreciation allows larger deductions relative to the accelerated schedule, thus balancing out some of the earlier revenue gains. This phenomenon is more prominent in asset classes that have longer lives. See Gravelle, "Reducing Depreciation Allowances."

26. CBO, *Reducing the Deficit*. Gravelle also analyzes the budget effects of CBO's proposal. The effect on the statutory tax rate is smaller than under the ADS proposal. See Gravelle, "Reducing Depreciation Allowances."

27. Depreciation lifetimes are currently 3, 5, 7, 10, 15, or 20 years. CBO's proposal would raise the lifetimes to 4, 8, 11, 20, 30, or 39 (most structures would be unaffected by this option). See CBO, *Reducing the Deficit*, 180.

28. Ibid., 180–81. CBO's proposal is only a temporary fix because tax rates would no longer be in parity when inflation changes in the future. A system could be imagined wherein depreciation schedules were indexed for inflation, but such a system would prove complex administratively. The 2.3 percent inflation rate from the consumer price index is from CBO, "The Budget and Economic Outlook: Fiscal Years 2013 to 2023," Washington, DC, February 2013, 5.

29. Entin, "Tax Treatment of Capital Assets," 10–11.

30. Ibid., 12.

31. Ibid., 10–11. Entin provides a full discussion of how the future value of depreciation write-offs alters the after-tax returns on investments.

32. CBO, "Taxing Capital Income: Effective Rates and Approaches to Reform," Washington, DC, October 2005.

33. Ibid. The effective rates cited under expensing also include removing contributions, eligibility, and withdrawal restrictions on retirement savings accounts. CBO's full analysis also removes interest deductions to get a zero effective rate on both debt- and equity-financed investments.

34. Curtis S. Dubay, "The Proper Tax Treatment of Interest," Backgrounder 2868, Heritage Foundation, Washington, DC, February 19, 2014.

35. Mackie estimates that intangibles have an effective rate of 4.4 percent, compared to rates of 30.5 and 38.8 percent for equipment and structures, respectively. See James B. Mackie, "Unfinished Business of the 1986 Tax Reform Act: An Effective Tax Rate Analysis of Current Issues in the Taxation of Capital Income," *National Tax Journal* 55, no. 2 (June 2002): 293–337, 310.

36. Entin, "Tax Treatment of Capital Assets," 18.

37. CBO, "Taxing Capital Income."

38. Ibid., 7–8.

39. CBO estimates inflation over the years 2013–23 to be 2.3 percent. See CBO, "Budget and Economic Outlook: Fiscal Years 2013 to 2023," 5. Entin suggests that competitive investments must earn back 3.0 to 3.5 percent. See Entin, "Tax Treatment of Capital Assets," 9.

40. This is the case for both straight-line and accelerated depreciation, although the effect is largest when cost recovery is longer.

41. Entin, "Tax Treatment of Capital Assets," 10–11.

42. JCT, "Background and Present Law," 47–59.

43. Ibid.

44. Matthew Mitchell, "The Pathology of Privilege: The Economic Consequences of Government Favoritism," Mercatus Center at George Mason University, Arlington, VA, July 2012, 11, 17–18.

45. Seth H. Giertz and Jacob Feldman, "The Costs of Tax Policy Uncertainty and the Need for Tax Reform," *Tax Notes* 138, no. 8 (February 25, 2013): 951–63.

46. This number includes individuals' and businesses' direct outlays, time spent on filing requirements and audits, and IRS administrative costs. It is estimated that businesses spent 2.94 billion hours complying with the federal tax code in 2008. See Arthur B. Laffer, Wayne H. Winegarden, and John Childs, "The Economic Burden Caused by Tax Code Complexity," Laffer Center, Austin, TX, April 2011, 3.

47. Ibid., 23.

48. Vernon L. Smith, "Tax Depreciation Policy and Investment Theory," *International Economic Review* 4, no. 1 (January 1963): 80–91, 91.

49. Alan J. Auerbach and Dale W. Jorgenson, "Inflation-Proof Depreciation of Assets," *Harvard Business Review* (September–October 1980): 113–18.

50. Duke–CFO Magazine Global Business Outlook Survey, September 2011.

51. Entin, "Tax Treatment of Capital Assets," 12.

52. Alan J. Auerbach, "A Modern Corporate Tax," Center for American Progress and Hamilton Project, Washington, DC, December 2010.

53. Entin, "Tax Treatment of Capital Assets," 13.

54. Because bonus depreciation was extended as part of the American Taxpayer Relief Act of 2012, many investments have used the 50 percent deduction. Previous years had bonus depreciation allowances of as much as 100 percent. See Ernst & Young, "Fiscal Cliff Legislation Extends 50% Bonus Depreciation and Leasing Provisions."

55. The transition costs arise because of a disruption in tax collection during the first year, when a business writes off the

entire investment. If a large portion of past investments has already been fully deducted, there will be less disruption in tax revenue during a transition from depreciation to expensing.

56. Schuyler, "Comparing the Growth and Revenue Effects of Four Proposed Depreciation Systems." Projections are from the Tax Foundation's "Taxes and Growth" model, with all results presented in steady state.

57. The data used are from IRS, "Table 12—Returns of Active Corporations, Other than Forms 1120-REIT, 1120-RIC, and 1120S" (1998–2012), June 27, 2014. These statistics do not include S corporations and other pass-through entities. Pass-through corporations are taxed differently.

58. Industry sensitivity to depreciation reform is measured by examining which industries would experience the largest increase in average effective tax rates if depreciation were removed as a deduction. These same businesses would likely have the most to gain from adopting expensing.

59. CBO, "Taxing Capital Income," 7–8.

60. Neubig's seven reasons are (a) expensing's timing benefit does not show up in the book effective tax rate, (b) many assets are already fully expensed, (c) corporations fear the removal of interest deductibility, (d) expensing does not reduce taxes on profits—a lower tax rate applies more broadly, (e) not all companies will be able to benefit from expensing immediately, (f) expensing reduces the tax wedge between tangible and intangible assets—a lower statutory rate would reduce the wedge for all corporate decisions, and (g) expensing does not reduce the fear that statutory rates may go up in the future. See Tom Neubig, "Where's the Applause? Why Most Corporations Prefer a Lower Rate," *Tax Notes* 111 (April 2006): 483–86.

61. J. D. Foster, "The Big Choice for Growth: Lower Tax Rates v. Expensing," *Tax Notes*, December 17, 2012.

62. Gravelle, "Reducing Depreciation Allowances."

63. Foster makes a similar argument when he claims that business leaders are more likely to support lower taxes than expensing if given the tradeoff. This chapter does not argue that expensing is the only necessary tax reform. A robust tax reform plan must fit many of these smaller reforms together. See J. D. Foster, "The Big Choice for Jobs and Growth: Lower Tax Rates versus Expensing," Backgrounder 2810, Heritage Foundation, Washington, DC, June 19, 2013.

64. Duke–CFO Magazine Global Business Outlook Survey.

65. Jesse Edgerton, "Investment, Accounting, and the Salience of the Corporate Income Tax," Working paper, Oxford University Centre for Business Taxation, Oxford, UK, October 2012.

66. Ibid.

67. David Hulse and Jane Livingstone, "Incentive Effects of Bonus Depreciation," *Journal of Accounting and Public Policy* 29, no. 6 (2010): 578–603.

68. Research from Eric Zwick and James Mahon of Harvard University finds significant positive effects of changes in accelerated depreciation policy. Most strikingly, they find bonus depreciation raised investment by 17.3 percent on average between 2001 and 2004 and by 29.5 percent between 2008 and 2010. The strong incentive found in this new research may be from the inclusion of small and medium firms, which are more responsive to tax incentives. See Eric Zwick and James Mahon, "Do Financial Frictions Amplify Fiscal Policy? Evidence from Business Investment Stimulus," Job Market Paper, Harvard University, Cambridge, MA, January 7, 2014.

69. Robert E. Hall and Dale W. Jorgenson, "Tax Policy and Investment Behavior," *American Economic Review* 57, no. 3 (June 1967): 391–414.

70. Hulse and Livingstone, "Incentive Effects of Bonus Depreciation."

71. Kevin A. Hassett and Gilbert E. Metcalf, "Investment with Uncertain Tax Policy: Does Random Tax Policy Discourage Investment?," *Economic Journal* 109 (July 1999): 372–93.

72. *Hearing on Extenders and Tax Reform: Seeking Long-Term Solutions before the United States Senate Committee on Finance*, 112th Cong., 2nd sess. (January 31, 2012) (testimony of Jason J. Fichtner, senior research fellow, Mercatus Center, "Increasing America's Competitiveness by Lowering the Corporate Tax Rate and Simplifying the Tax Code").

73. Auerbach, "Modern Corporate Tax," 12. See also Schuyler, "Comparing the Growth and Revenue Effects of Four Proposed Depreciation Systems."

74. Entin, "Tax Treatment of Capital Assets," 19.

CHAPTER 6: WHY SHOULD CONGRESS REFORM THE MORTGAGE INTEREST DEDUCTION?

1. Edward L. Glaeser and Jesse M. Shapiro, "The Benefits of the Home Mortgage Interest Deduction," in *Tax Policy and the Economy*, vol. 17, ed. James M. Poterba (Cambridge, MA: MIT Press, 2003), 37–82.

2. Jonathan Skinner and Daniel Feenberg, "The Impact of the 1986 Tax Reform Act on Personal Saving," NBER Working Paper 3257, National Bureau of Economic Research, Washington, DC, February 1990. See also Dean M. Maki, "Household Debt and the Tax Reform Act of 1986," *American Economic Review* 91, no. 1 (March 2001): 305–19.

3. President's Advisory Panel on Federal Tax Reform, "Simple, Fair, and Pro-growth: Proposals to Fix America's Tax System," November 2005, figure 5.5.

4. Alan D. Viard and Robert Carroll, *Progressive Consumption Taxation: The X-Tax Revisited* (Washington, DC: AEI Press, 2012).

5. Rick Judson, "Keep Homeowners' Tax Deductions: Opposing View," *USA Today*, April 2, 2013.

6. Jeffrey M. Jones, "Americans Oppose Eliminating Income Tax Deductions," Gallup, April 15, 2011. See also IRS, "2010 Estimated Data Line Counts Individual Income Tax Returns," Rev. 11-2012, Washington, DC.

7. Office of Management and Budget, *Analytical Perspectives: Budget of the United States Government, Fiscal Year 2015* (Washington, DC: Government Printing House), March 4, 2014, table 14-1, 206.

8. The standard deduction serves two important roles: to sim-plify the federal tax code and to favor lower-income taxpayers by making the tax code more progressive. Part of the design of the standard deduction is to render it unnecessary for some taxpayers to track their tax-related expenditures throughout the year, because the cumulative effort would not exceed the standard deduction. For millions of taxpayers, simply claim-ing the standard deduction saves time and resources. However, the standard deduction is also designed to reduce the taxable income of low-income taxpayers, regardless of whether any tax-related expenditures have been incurred. (Along these lines, tax-related expenditures might be viewed as having gone to waste. In short, in a world where there must be tax-favored spending, it seems that increasing the number of low- and middle-income housing units would reap more social benefits than an equal amount of money in tax subsidies given to high-income earners.)

9. Glaeser and Shapiro, "Benefits of the Home Mortgage Interest Deduction."

10. David C. Ling and Gary A. McGill, "Evidence on the Demand for Mortgage Debt by Owner-Occupants," *Journal of Urban Economics* 44, no. 3 (1998): 391–414. See also James R. Follain and Lisa Sturman Melamed, "The False Messiah of Tax Policy:

What Elimination of the Home Mortgage Interest Deduction Promises and a Careful Look at What It Delivers," *Journal of Housing Research* 9, no. 2 (March 2000): 179–99.

11. John E. Anderson, Jeffrey Clemens, and Andrew Hanson, "Capping the Mortgage Interest Deduction," *National Tax Journal* 60, no. 4 (December 2007): 769–85. See also Harvey S. Rosen, "Housing Decisions and the U.S. Income Tax: An Econometric Analysis," *Journal of Public Economics* 11, no. 1 (February 1979): 1–23.

12. Richard K. Green and Andrew Reschovsky, "The Design of a Mortgage Interest Tax Credit," final report submitted to the National Housing Institute, Orange, NJ, September 1997.

13. Authors' calculations based on data from Adrian Dungan and Michael Parisi, "Individual Income Tax Returns, Preliminary Data, 2010," *SOI Bulletin* 31, no. 3 (Winter 2012): 5–18, 6–8, figure A. An inflation-adjusted income of $100,000 in 1997 would be approximately $136,000 in 2010. Unfortunately, more specific data on MID use could not be obtained. IRS data examine adjusted gross income only in a distribution ranging from $100,000 to $200,000.

14. Will Fischer and Chye-Ching Huang, "Mortgage Interest Deduction Is Ripe for Reform: Conversion to Tax Credit Could Raise Revenue and Make Subsidy More Effective and Fairer," Center on Budget and Policy Priorities, Washington, DC, June 25, 2013.

15. David C. Ling and Gary A. McGill, "The Variation of Homeowner Tax Preferences by Income, Age and Leverage," *Real Estate Economics* 35, no. 4 (2007): 505–39.

16. Robert J. Shiller, "Owning a Home Isn't Always a Virtue," *New York Times*, July 13, 2013.

17. Calvin H. Johnson, "Was It Lost? Personal Deductions under Tax Reform," *SMU Law Review* 59, no. 2 (August 23, 2006): 689–720.

18. Stanley S. Surrey, *Pathways to Tax Reform: The Concept of Tax Expenditures* (Cambridge, MA: Harvard University Press, 1973).

19. Peter Brady, Julie-Anne Cronin, and Scott Houser, "Regional Differences in the Utilization of the Mortgage Interest Deduction," *Public Finance Review* 31, no. 4 (2003): 327–66.

20. James R. Follain and David C. Ling, "The Federal Tax Subsidy to Housing and the Reduced Value of the Mortgage Interest Deduction," *National Tax Journal* 44, no. 2 (June 1991): 147–68.

21. Dungan and Parisi, "Individual Income Tax Returns, Preliminary Data, 2010."

22. Follain and Ling, "Federal Tax Subsidy to Housing." Although the alternative minimum tax limits the deductibility of all itemized deductions for some high-income taxpayers, there is still some benefit to itemizing and claiming the MID. The regular income tax allows a taxpayer to deduct mortgage interest from a primary residence on the primary mortgage as well as interest on a home equity line of credit (up to $100,000 of a loan's value). Under the alternative minimum tax, however, the interest on home equity is disallowed; the primary mortgage is allowed but is limited.

23. Todd Sinai and Joseph Gyourko, "The (Un)changing Geographical Distribution of Housing Tax Benefits: 1980 to 2000," in *Tax Policy and the Economy*, vol. 18, ed. James Poterba, 175–208 (Cambridge, MA: MIT Press, 2004). See also US Census Bureau, "Median Household Income (in 2012 Inflation-Adjusted Dollars) by State Ranked from Highest to Lowest Using 3-Year Average: 2010–2012," http://www .census.gov/hhes/www/income/data/incpovhlth/2012 /stateonline_12.xls.

24. Joseph Gyourko and Todd Sinai, "Spatial Distribution of Mortgage Deduction Benefits across and within Metropolitan Areas in the United States," in *Using Tax Policy to Increase Homeownership among Low- and Moderate-Income Households*, ed. Richard K. Green and Andrew Reschovsky, 137–86 (New York: Ford Foundation, 2001).

25. Green and Reschovsky, "Design of a Mortgage Interest Tax Credit," 72.

26. Donald Morris and Jing Wang, "How and Why States Use the Home Mortgage Interest Deduction," *Tax Notes* 64 (June 4, 2012): 697–713. The specific policy reason for this statistical anomaly in Alabama is unclear. However, the state of Alabama has a very low standard deduction amount, which likely results in more people itemizing deductions on their state income tax returns compared to other states. The data used come from the IRS tables referenced in Morris and Wang's paper.

27. James M. Poterba and Todd Sinai, "Revenue Costs and Incentive Effects of the Mortgage Interest Deduction for Owner-Occupied Housing," *National Tax Journal* 62, no. 2, part 2 (June 2011): 531–64.

28. Ling and McGill, "Evidence on the Demand for Mortgage Debt by Owner-Occupants."

29. Green and Reschovsky, "Design of a Mortgage Interest Tax Credit."

30. Glaeser and Shapiro, "Benefits of the Home Mortgage Interest Deduction."

31. Thomas P. Boehm and Alan M. Schlottmann, "Market Conditions and Housing Choices: A Comparison of Homeownership across Three Decades," *Real Estate Economics* 39 (2011): 547–600.

32. Richard K. Green and Michelle J. White, "Measuring the Benefits of Homeowning: Effects on Children," *Journal of Urban Economics* 41, no. 3 (1997): 441–61.

33. This calculation assumes each household has one child. The benefit is higher with an increased number of children.

34. Glaeser and Shapiro, "Benefits of the Home Mortgage Interest Deduction."

35. Richard Voith, "Does the Federal Tax Treatment of Housing Affect the Pattern of Metropolitan Development?," *Federal Reserve Bank of Philadelphia Business Review*, March–April 1999, 3–16.

36. Henry J. Aaron, *Shelter and Subsidies: Who Benefits from Federal Housing Policies?* (Washington, DC: Brookings Institution, 1972); Harvey S. Rosen and Kenneth T. Rosen, "Federal Taxes and Homeownership: Evidence from Time Series," *Journal of Political Economy* 88, no. 1 (February 1980): 59–75; Harvey S. Rosen, "Housing Behavior and the Experimental Housing Allowance Program: What Have We Learned?," NBER Working Paper 657, National Bureau of Economic Research, Washington, DC, May 1985; James M. Poterba, "Tax Subsidies to Owner-Occupied Housing: An Asset-Market Approach," *Quarterly Journal of Economics* 99, no. 4 (November 1984): 729–52; James M. Poterba, "Taxation and Housing: Old Questions, New Answers," *American Economic Review* 82, no. 2 (May 1992): 237–42; Edwin S. Mills, "Dividing Up the Investment Pie: Have We Overinvested in Housing?," *Federal Reserve Bank of Philadelphia Business Review* (March–April 1987): 13–23.

37. Anderson, Clemens, and Hanson, "Capping the Mortgage Interest Deduction." See also Rosen, "Housing Decisions and the U.S. Income Tax."

38. Green and Reschovsky, "Design of a Mortgage Interest Tax Credit."

39. Skinner and Feenberg, "Impact of the 1986 Tax Reform Act."

40. Maki, "Household Debt and the Tax Reform Act of 1986."

41. Poterba and Sinai, "Revenue Costs and Incentive Effects."

42. Follain and Melamed, "False Messiah of Tax Policy." See also Martin Gervais and Manish Pandey, "Who Cares about

Mortgage Interest Deductibility?," *Canadian Public Policy* 34, no. 1 (2008): 1461–89; William Gale, Jonathan Gruber, and Seth Stephens-Davidowitz, "Encouraging Homeownership through the Tax Code," *Tax Notes* 115, no. 12 (June 18, 2007): 1171–89; Poterba and Sinai, "Revenue Costs and Incentive Effects."

43. Office of Management and Budget, *Analytical Perspectives, Budget of the United States Government, Fiscal Year 2015.*

44. Lawrence Yun, "Why the MID Deserves to Stay," *Realtor Mag*, September 2010. See also Dennis R. Capozza, Richard Green, and Patric H. Hendershott, "Taxes, Mortgage Borrowing, and Residential Land Prices," in *Economic Effects of Fundamental Tax Reform*, ed. Henry J. Aaron and William G. Gale, 171–210 (Washington, DC: Brookings Institution Press, 1996).

45. Yun, "Why the MID Deserves to Stay."

46. Anderson, Clemens, and Hanson, "Capping the Mortgage Interest Deduction." See also Rosen, "Housing Decisions and the U.S. Income Tax."

47. Andrew Hanson, "Size of Home, Homeownership, and the Mortgage Interest Deduction," *Journal of Housing Economics* 21, no. 3 (September 2012): 195–210.

48. Glaeser and Shapiro, "Benefits of the Home Mortgage Interest Deduction."

49. Andrew Hanson, "The Incidence of the Mortgage Interest Deduction: Evidence from the Market for Home Purchase Loans," *Public Finance Review* 40, no. 3 (May 2012): 339–59.

50. Because of higher statutory tax rates at the time, the US tax code encouraged more investment in homeownership. When the statutory rate was lowered, tax loopholes such as the MID were less useful in minimizing taxes. See Follain and Ling, "Federal Tax Subsidy to Housing."

51. Ibid.

52. Authors' calculations using US Bureau of Labor statistics and CPI Inflation Calculator.

53. Green and Reschovsky, "Design of a Mortgage Interest Tax Credit." Inflation adjustment is the authors' calculation.

54. Ibid.

55. National Commission on Fiscal Responsibility and Reform, "The Moment of Truth," Washington, DC, December 2010.

56. Anderson, Clemens, and Hanson, "Capping the Mortgage Interest Deduction."

57. President's Advisory Panel on Federal Tax Reform, "Simple, Fair, and Pro-growth."

58. Ling and McGill, "Variation of Homeowner Tax Preferences."

59. James R. Follain, David C. Ling, and Gary A. McGill, "The Preferential Income Tax Treatment of Owner-Occupied Housing: Who Really Benefits?," *Housing Policy Debate* 4, no. 1 (March 1993): 1–24.

60. Amanda Eng, Harvey Galper, Georgia Ivsin, and Eric Toder, "Options to Reform the Deduction for Home Mortgage Interest," Urban Institute–Brookings Institution Tax Policy Center, Washington, DC, March 18, 2013.

61. Adam C. Carasso, Eugene Steuerle, and Elizabeth Bell, "Making Tax Incentives for Homeownership More Equitable and Efficient," Discussion Paper 21, Urban Institute, Washington, DC, 2005.

62. Peter Dreier, "The New Politics of Housing: How to Rebuild the Constituency for a Progressive Federal Housing Policy," *Journal of the American Planning Association* 63, no. 1 (November 27, 2007): 5–27.

63. Richard K. Green, and Kerry D. Vandell, "Giving Households Credit: How Changes in the U.S. Tax Code Could Promote Homeownership," *Regional Science and Urban Economics* 29, no. 4 (1999): 419–44.

64. Ling and McGill, "Variation of Homeowner Tax Preferences."

65. Matthew Chambers, Carlos Garriga, and Don E. Schlagenhauf, "Housing Policy and the Progressivity of Income Taxation," *Journal of Monetary Economics* 56, no. 8 (November 2009): 1116–34.

66. A neutral tax system would not allow the deduction of interest by the borrower if the interest were not taxable income to the lender. Hence, some have argued that the MID should not be eliminated because the interest earned on the loan is taxable to lenders. For example, Curtis Dubay argues that when considering tax reform proposals, "Congress should never eliminate tax deductions simply to raise revenue. If it decides to reform the tax code, it should establish a neutral tax base. This means that as long as it taxes interest income to lenders, it should keep interest deductible to borrowers." See Curtis S. Dubay, "The Proper Tax Treatment of Interest," Backgrounder 2868, Heritage Foundation, Washington, DC, February 19, 2014. We are inclined to agree but suggest that the perverse incentives caused by the MID require reform. Although fundamental tax reform is outside the scope of this chapter, we would support removing the taxation of interest income and capital gains, along with removing the deductibility of interest income by the borrower, not only as a means

of adhering to a neutral tax system but also as a means to increase saving, investment, and economic growth.

67. Ling and McGill, "Variation of Homeowner Tax Preferences."

68. Follain and Melamed, "False Messiah of Tax Policy."

69. Poterba and Sinai, "Revenue Costs and Incentive Effects."

70. Anderson, Clemens, and Hanson, "Capping the Mortgage Interest Deduction." See also Rosen, "Housing Decisions and the U.S. Income Tax."

71. To avoid potential gaming of the credit, it would only apply to primary residences with a mortgage. It would not be available for second homes or for home equity lines of credit.

72. Green and Reschovsky, "Design of a Mortgage Interest Tax Credit."

73. Authors' calculations. According to the US Census Bureau's most recent 2009 data on mortgages, there are 76.4 million owner-occupied homes with mortgages in the United States. See US Census Bureau, *The 2012 Statistical Abstract: The National Data Book* (Washington, DC, 2012), table 998. In 2013, $69 billion was spent on the home mortgage interest deduction. See Office of Management and Budget, *Analytical Perspectives: Budget of the United States Government, Fiscal Year 2015*, 206.

74. Jason J. Fichtner and Jacob M. Feldman, "The Hidden Costs of Tax Compliance," Mercatus Center at George Mason University, Arlington, VA, May 20, 2013. See also Jason J. Fichtner and Jacob M. Feldman, "When Are Tax Expenditures Really Spending? A Look at Tax Expenditures and Lessons from the Tax Reform Act of 1986," Mercatus Working Paper 11-45, Mercatus Center at George Mason University, Arlington, VA, November 2011.

CHAPTER 7: HOW DO PEOPLE RESPOND TO THE MARRIAGE TAX PENALTY?

1. James R. Alm and Mikhail I. Melnik, "Taxing the 'Family' in the Individual Income Tax," Andrew Young School of Policy Studies, Georgia State University, Atlanta, July 2004, 19.

2. Married couples must choose to file either a joint return ("married filing jointly") or a separate return ("married filing separately"). But using the "married filing separately" status is not the same as filing as an unmarried person. The "married filing separately" status is generally the least beneficial filing status because the two taxpayers are not allowed to claim all the deductions and credits that are allowed otherwise.

Furthermore, the income level at which the 25 percent, 28 percent, 33 percent, 35 percent, and 39.6 percent marginal tax rates begin to apply are lower for "married filing separately" than when filing either as an unmarried person or as "married filing jointly," an obvious tax penalty.

3. Daniel R. Feenberg and Harvey S. Rosen, "Recent Developments in the Marriage Tax," NBER Working Paper 4705, National Bureau of Economic Research, Cambridge, MA, April 1994, 15.

4. Sara LaLumia, "The Effects of Joint Taxation of Married Couples on Labor Supply and Non-wage Income," *Journal of Public Economics* 92, no. 7 (July 2008): 1698–1719, 1700.

5. Florence Guy Seabury, letter to the editor, *New York Times*, May 25, 1942.

6. *The Economist*, "We Did It!," December 30, 2009. See also Jonathan House, "Women Reach a Milestone in Job Market," *Wall Street Journal*, November 20, 2013.

7. Leslie A. Whittington and James Alm, "Tax Reductions, Tax Changes, and the Marriage Penalty," *National Tax Journal* 54, no. 3 (September 2001): 455–72. See also James Alm and Leslie A. Whittington, "Shacking Up or Shelling Out: Income Taxes, Marriage, and Cohabitation," *Review of Economics of the Household* 1, no. 3 (2003): 169–86.

8. The EITC is a federal tax credit for low- to moderate-income individuals and married couples. The credit predominantly applies to filers with one or more dependent children and has three different phaseout schedules for one, two, and three or more children. Many two-earner couples would experience a diminished credit if married because the delay in schedule phaseout is not double the single-filer credit.

9. For example, see Laura Wheaton, "Low-Income Families and the Marriage Tax," Policy Brief, Urban Institute, Washington, DC, September 1998; Robert I. Lerman, "How Do Marriage, Cohabitation, and Single Parenthood Affect the Material Hardships of Families with Children?," US Department of Health and Human Services, Washington, DC, July 2002; and Heather J. Bachman, Rebekah Levine Coley, and P. Lindsay Chase-Lansdale, "Is Maternal Marriage Beneficial for Low-Income Adolescents?," *Applied Developmental Science* 13, no. 4 (2009): 153–71.

10. LaLumia, "Effects of Joint Taxation of Married Couples," 1699.

11. Michael Bar and Oksana Leukhina, "To Work or Not to Work: Did Tax Reforms Affect Labor Force Participation of Married

Couples?," *B.E. Journal of Macroeconomics* 9, no. 1 (2009): 1–23.

12. Nada Eissa and Hilary Williamson Hoynes, "Explaining the Fall and Rise in the Tax Cost of Marriage: The Effect of Tax Laws and Demographic Trends, 1984–1997," *National Tax Journal* 53, no. 3, part 2 (September 2000): 683–711, 685.

13. Whittington and Alm, "Tax Reductions, Tax Changes, and the Marriage Penalty," 469. See also Kyle Pomerleau, "Understanding the Marriage Penalty and Marriage Bonus," Tax Foundation, Washington, DC, April 23, 2015.

14. Feenberg and Rosen, "Recent Developments in the Marriage Tax."

15. Ibid., 10.

16. Eissa and Hoynes, "Explaining the Fall and Rise in the Tax Cost of Marriage," 686–88.

17. Feenberg and Rosen, "Recent Developments in the Marriage Tax," 15.

18. Eissa and Hoynes, "Explaining the Fall and Rise in the Tax Cost of Marriage," 684.

19. Ibid., 704.

20. Whittington and Alm, "Tax Reductions, Tax Changes, and the Marriage Penalty," 456.

21. These reforms were included in the Economic Growth and Tax Relief Reconciliation Act of 2001 and the Jobs and Growth Tax Relief Reconciliation Act of 2003.

22. Whittington and Alm, "Tax Reductions, Tax Changes, and the Marriage Penalty," 458.

23. Frederick J. Feucht, L. Murphy Smith, and Robert H. Strawser, "The Negative Effect of the Marriage Penalty Tax on American Society," *Academy of Accounting and Financial Studies Journal* 13, no. 1 (2009): 103–25, 104–5, quoting remarks made by President Bush.

24. Whittington and Alm, "Tax Reductions, Tax Changes, and the Marriage Penalty," 459.

25. Ibid., 470.

26. Hayley Fisher, "The Health Benefits of Marriage: Evidence Using Variation in Marriage Tax Penalties," Working Paper, Cambridge University, Cambridge, UK, November 2010, 19.

27. Stacy Dickert-Conlin, "Taxes and Transfers: Their Effects on the Decision to End a Marriage," *Journal of Public Economics* 73, no. 2 (August 1999): 217–40.

28. Ibid., 234.

29. Ibid., 230.

30. Ibid.

31. Feenberg and Rosen, "Recent Developments in the Marriage Tax," 7. This example is specific to a couple in which each earner receives $10,000 per year in income with two dependent children after the 1993 tax reform act.

32. Dickert-Conlin, "Taxes and Transfers," 221.

33. Bar and Leukhina, "To Work or Not to Work?," 2.

34. Eissa and Hoynes, "Explaining the Fall and Rise in the Tax Cost of Marriage," 683.

35. Ibid., 685.

36. Bar and Leukhina, "To Work or Not to Work?," 3.

37. Ibid., 14.

38. Alm and Whittington, "Shacking Up or Shelling Out," 16.

39. Joint Economic Committee, "Reducing Marriage Taxes: Issues and Proposals," Washington, DC, May 1998.

40. A form of income splitting already exists in the United States. However, it applies only to owners of profitable small corporations paying themselves under categorizations of employee salaries and bonuses. Some researchers argue that the expanded brackets for joint filers are a form of income splitting. This chapter refers to potential income splitting in the context of direct proportionality to the "single" tax bracket.

41. Stephen Matthews, "Trends in Top Incomes and Their Tax Policy Implications," OECD Taxation Working Paper 4, Organisation for Economic Co-operation and Development, Paris, November 3, 2011, 37.

42. Joint Economic Committee, "Reducing Marriage Taxes," 8.

43. Whittington and Alm, "Tax Reductions, Tax Changes, and the Marriage Penalty," 472.

44. Eissa and Hoynes, "Explaining the Fall and Rise in the Tax Cost of Marriage," 685.

CONCLUSION: KEY PRINCIPLES FOR SUCCESSFUL, SUSTAINABLE TAX REFORM

1. As noted in the introduction to this book, meeting the government's spending requirements is not a mandate to raise taxes to higher levels to support even higher levels of government spending. Although good tax reform will increase economic growth and such growth will increase tax revenue to some extent, the United States spends more money than it collects

and needs to reduce its spending. Discussions on how the federal government should reduce spending are outside the scope of this book, but interested readers looking for ideas can start here: Jason Fichtner, "The 1 Percent Solution," Mercatus Working Paper 11-05, Mercatus Center at George Mason University, Arlington, VA, February 2011.

ABOUT THE AUTHORS

Jason J. Fichtner is a senior research fellow at the Mercatus Center at George Mason University. He has served in several positions at the Social Security Administration, including deputy commissioner of social security (acting), chief economist, and associate commissioner for retirement policy. He also served as senior economist with the Joint Economic Committee of the US Congress, as senior consultant with the Office of Federal Tax Services of Arthur Andersen LLP in Washington, DC, and as an economist with the Research Division of the Internal Revenue Service. Fichtner earned his BA from the University of Michigan, Ann Arbor; his MPP from Georgetown University; and his PhD in Public Administration and Policy from Virginia Tech. He serves on the adjunct faculty at the Georgetown McCourt School of Public Policy, the Johns Hopkins School of Advanced International Studies, and the Virginia Tech Center for Public Administration and Policy.

Jacob M. Feldman is an economist at the US Bureau of Labor Statistics. He specialized in the economics of federal taxation as a research analyst at the Mercatus

Center and as the Thomas Jefferson Fellow at Americans for Tax Reform. He received his MA in economics from George Mason University and his BA in economics and Jewish studies from the University of Virginia.

Co-author of chapter 3
Nicholas J. Tuszynski participated in the Presidential Management Fellows program from 2012 to 2014 and has held positions at the Department of Transportation and the Texas Public Policy Foundation. He received his MA in economics from George Mason University and his BBA in economics from Loyola University New Orleans. Tuszynski currently works in the federal government focusing on budget execution, portfolio risk analysis, and financial planning.

Co-author of chapter 5
Adam N. Michel is a program coordinator for the Spending and Budget Initiative at the Mercatus Center. He received his MA in economics from George Mason University and is an alumnus of the Mercatus MA Fellowship program. Michel graduated from Whitman College with a BA in politics. He previously worked at the Tax Foundation as a federal tax policy intern. Michel has also worked on labor policy as a research associate at the Competitive Enterprise Institute.

INDEX

Page numbers in *italics* denote tables and figures.